By the same author
CASTRA AETERNA
ACHTER HET PANTSER
GODENJACHT
TOOGHANGER
ALIBI KONING

Trump's Battle

By

CORNELIS BROUWER

Colofon

Copyright 2016 Cornelis Brouwer

ISBN-13: **978-1540743985**

ISBN-10: **1540743985**

Table of Contents

PREFACE

The election of Donald Trump as 45th President of the United States of America caused an atmosphere of insecurity throughout the political establishment in the world. In particular the leaders of the European countries and those of the European Union were unpleasantly surprised. Without exception, all those political leaders were prepared to salute Hillary Clinton, their favorite, as the new President of the United States. Forgotten were the disgusting family details of the Clinton family and the by the concerned governments excessively controlled public media praised the woman into heaven and relegated Donald Trump to the dung-hill. According to the public media and the European politicians in general, he was unpredictable, blunt, an unbelievable lack of political knowledge, unreliable with a questionable background and career as businessman. But most of all was feared the fact that he was not a politician. That fact led to remarks from EU-politicians and those from, in particular The Netherlands and Germany that are worth to be commented.

The website of The White House offers subscribers the possibility to comment on articles on the website and offers the possibility to bring ideas from those subscribers under the attention of the President. Most of the governments in the world, including the Kremlin, do the same. But my experience is, that no reaction follows and to the contents is not paid any attention. We may conclude that contacting The White House in this way is as useful as carrying water to the sea. But sometimes a directly to a head of state addressed letter causes the desired reactions, as the reader will see.

In view of the lack of experience of President Trump with politics, and in particular European politics, according to some distasteful European politicians, some enlightenment may help him to adjust to the right attitude in case he has to meet with them. It is my pleasure to help him adapting the right attitude in those cases and prevent him from ordering one of his accompanying US Marines to beat those European swindlers out of The White House with a baseball bat.

Still knowing my staff work, up to the highest level, very well and aware of the fact that the appropriate letter would end in the round archive after being opened by the postal clerk, I decided publishing my thoughts in this book. Together with self explanatory letters to former President G.W. Busch and former UK PM Blair, which also may serve as guidelines for excellent presidency.

Cornelis Brouwer

WO1, RNLA (retired)

CHAPTER 1

The challenges

The term 'politician', once a man or woman who, driven by ideals, knowledge, dedication and insight used to pursue a prosperous country with a prosperous population with the highest ethical values. This now rather old-fashioned pursuit no longer exists. The old-fashioned sense of the word politician either. And that announces itself to end of the meaning of democracy. Politicians now are people who only use the word democracy once every four years. That's when elections are held in which they should, and will, make every effort to be (re)elected. Their rather large earnings are indeed at stake. So, once every four years, the street scene is marked by all sorts of people who try a shot at the excessively high salaries and parliamentary allowances. With an effort that better be used for other goals, drooling, slithering and slipping on their own body secretions politicians of various political directions rush from election meetings to attend party meetings and even house to house visits to win as many votes as possible. And at every critical question they produce a satisfactory answer for the questioner. Until the day of the actual elections. Each citizen is then appealed to his moral duty to participate in the democratic process and thus to vote and give substance and support to the constitution and the parliamentary system. Good citizens, totally blinded by the promises that they will become filthy rich after the election, never have to work again and his or her children can be delivered at the nursery to receive an education in uniformity, the voters step into the voting facility and cross the box of those who promised golden mountains. As soon as the polling stations are closed, democracy ceases to exist. From then on, politicians and political parties are not approachable anymore and bringing their election promises and oath into memory is impossible. In the headquarters of the political parties, the computers are programmed with the well-known small program that puts all incoming e-mails from strangers automatically in the "blocked senders" list and emails are answered at best with an e-mail beginning with: noreply@ and of which the text reads: ´Your question has our attention and will be handled with care. We ask your understanding that we receive so many mails that makes it impossible to answer all senders individually.´

The procedure is common use in Germany and the Netherlands. Although I have no experience with elections and contacts with politicians in any US city, neither with those in Fotchdorf in Germany or Cuntvillage in Scotland, I can imagine that the situation is the same in that places.

Democracy may be considered to be the most abused word in this world.

For Donald Trump, being blamed to have no political experience, but must have a vast experience in politics being a normal voter, it will be a challenge to attract the interest of the American population to restore the real meaning of democracy in the United States. And somehow, by his attitude and practical view on his country concerning economy, defense of the interests of the United States and military defense against foreign politics and interests, I believe he can make it. But I would advise him not to use the phrase "Yes, we can". That phrase is loaded with disappointment and deception. Would I be Donald Trump, the phrase would be "All right. Let´s do it now".

The first challenge is to make it clear to both the US politicians and those in the world that talks with him always are accompanied by a secretary and using a lie detector of the Truster type. It proves in the first place that he sees the involvement of the public in his policy as an important task. Secondly, it prevents all kinds of foreign visitors, who are accustomed to the pubs diplomacy of the Third Reich and later on adapted by the EU, to make proposals that may be of interest for himself, but harmful to the population of the United States. Thirdly, it expresses the direct method of Donald Trump's idea of taking care of the interests of the United States to the population. Would that be rude to the visitor? Well, that visitor should not come up with camouflaged bribery in the first place.

The second challenge will be the choice of advisors. Good advisers are indispensable. But an opinion accompanied by a right motivation Donald Trump would not dare to present to the public for review, is not a good advice. It would be, after obtaining advice and possibly a second opinion on the same subject by experts, a prove of courage to invite four (Arbitrary. It may also be two or six and depending on the topic) ordinary working citizens to the White House and, after the subject being explained to them, give their opinion. Depending on their preference, their opinion should be anonymous. My experience taught me that often seemingly complicated problems presented to laymen, yielded simple solutions that were workable very well.

The third challenge Donald Trump has to face is to welcome European politicians in The White House. Many of them expressed their disgust about his nomination to the highest position in the United States in such a way that, would they have said that straight in his face, they probably were knocked down immediately. Now his election is final and he will be the 45th President of the United States, all of them as far as they likely have to meet him personally, stumble over their own feet in order to minimalize their often offending opinion.

A list of undesirable politicians and heads of state from the European Union and some individual European countries, available at the secretariat of the White House, would be necessary to prevent the politician involved, on arrival at The White House, be beaten out by a US Marine. But as far as it concerns the list, it is my pleasure to assist in preparing it.

The fourth challenge Donald Trump has to face, and maybe the most difficult, is removing a religious entity and all the subjects that are obedient to that religion, from the territory of the United States. The Constitution of the United States of America is not compatible with that religion. The challenge for Donald Trump lies in breaking all contacts with all countries where this religion is the state religion. Donald Trump can thereby ask whether he wants to shake the hand of a head of state that maintains the obnoxious habit of stoning, beheading, hanging and flogging to be used as punishment for acts that, in the United States, are not even offenses. Also for this subject I am glad giving a helping hand. But inviting an old veteran of the First or second Gulf War to enlighten the new President would very likely be helpful.

The fifth challenge is giving content to Donald Trump's promise: Make America great again.

The people of the Unites States, as those in any other country, has its own territory within clear marked borders, its own language, its own habits, manners and way of life. One of the, the people of the United States best describing slogans is: Land of the Free and Home of the Brave. By now, we could change that into: Land of the deceived and home of the abused. As will be proved later, the United States was lured into the role of policeman of the world and defender of freedom and democracy in a slow political process that ended in a United States, detested in vast parts of the world by many people. Making America great again means for me, Donald Trump: America comes in the first place, followed by the second, the third, the fourth, the fifth and the sixth place after which a row of nothings and then again America comes in the first place. Make America great again also means that all resources, brought up by the American population should be used for the well being of that population, the defense of the United States and its interests.

CHAPTER 2

The best way for Donald Trump to learn how European politics are executed is not a two years travel through the world and Europe as Mr. Juncker, President of the EU Commission, suggested. Reading The Rotten Heart of Europe may do. And that only takes thirty minutes.

The Rotten Heart of Europe

If one decision in the past turned out to be the worst ever in the history of the European Community, it was probably the choice of Brussels as 'Capital' of the European Union.

This choice brought politicians from all EU-countries direct into a political environment of a country that is known for its lack of loyalty towards the most important organizations it is a member of, its known political and juridical corruption and its parasitic behavior. In such an environment with its model function it is not amazing that, according to the Belgian newspaper Het Laatste Nieuws, 20 percent of all European representatives sign in for the presence at meetings, for which they get 200 Euro, to disappear after signing in. Another word for that behavior is called fraud. Are they to blame? Is a young teenage prostitute to be blamed when being grown up in the brothel of her mother?

Is it honest to blame several Belgian politicians for their corruption? Not really. The political environment, developed in a situation in which the French speaking Wallonia part of Belgium financially preys on the Dutch speaking Flemish part and the biggest political party, the socialist Parti Socialiste (PS) in Wallonia and the Socialist Party (PS) in Flanders filled for years the most important ministries, causes in fact the perfect conditions in which personal gain becomes the main motivation for Belgian politicians. Being a politician in Belgium is not an ideological call but a way to gain money by the many additional jobs that are offered. A good example is the Christian-democrat Mr. Jean-Luc Dehaene. The list of official additional jobs he executes may be called formidable with as top of the bill his role in the Dexia Bank with an annual remuneration of 1 million Euro. A sum that, once brought to the attention of the newspaper readers, caused bitter comments which Mr. Dehaene called populist because 1 million Euros was a normal wage for his position in the bank. But why should enterprises, banks and other money making organizations offer a politician an additional job? And at such a price? Is it because they believe to have contracted an excellent lobbyist? Maybe too excellent because in view of a lawsuit, filed against the top of the Dexia Bank including Dehaene in Paris, he may lose his parliamentary immunity to be charged. Significant for Belgium to have a representative in the EU of which the moral qualities are doubted by a French judge.

In Belgium, 9000 politicians, functioning on every level of government, possess one or more additional jobs. In 2008, 650 of them refused to report their jobs. Although they make themselves subject to prosecution, Minister of Justice, Mr. de Clerck, does not seem to be willing to enforce the concerning law. Of course not. One who is not capable of executing his task as Minister of Justice is hardly in a position to have other politicians being prosecuted. His moral suffering was greatly intensified when the Federal Juridical Police in Brussels informed the Mr. De Clerck of a sentence file against high magistrates in Brussels. That reported the newspaper De Tijd. The police force has indications that both the Prosecutor General in Brussels as well as the Prosecutor General of the Court of Cassation protected the suspected magistrates. For the investigators of Brussels the only solution was to send the file to the Minister of Justice. Well-informed sources speak about a system of corruption and book counterfeiting within the magistracy in Brussels. This coming to light, the consequences on the credibility of the magistracy would be dramatic. That confirmed several sources according to De Tijd. The investigation was already running for years, including the period in which Mr. Verhofstadt was PM. The interesting question that arises is: Would any police force dare not to inform the PM about the investigation against judges of the highest Courts of a country? Would the PM dare to keep that information for him and not bring it to the attention of the Ministerial Council? Would a PM not have informed his successor, Mr. Leterme? Would Mr. Leterme not have informed his successor, Mr. Van Rompuy? Obviously this three PM's in row posses a very big carpet in their offices. Corruption, the wide spread phenomenon in Belgium, is brought to the knowledge of the world when Willy Claes, the Flemish Belgian socialist and Secretary General of NATO, was forced to resign in 1995. His involvement in the Augusta corruption case led to his political ruin. Typical for Belgium is that none of the involved PS and SP politicians ever saw a prison from the inside. A penalty of 1500 Euro, three years of prison sentence conditional and a five year denial to execute any political job was all he and the top of the PS got. And this is what also the other involved politicians got. The only politician of all, involved in the Augusta case, who escaped any corrective measure was the last Belgian Minister of Education Vandenbroucke. In 1994 Vandenbroucke had to resign as foreign minister and in 1996 he also resigned from parliament due to his involvement in the Augusta scandal. He acknowledged that he was confronted with millions of Belgian francs which came as bribery money from the Italian helicopter builder Augusta. He advised his staff-party members to "have the money burned" if necessary. Vandenbroucke was never prosecuted destroying material evidence of a crime but took a voluntary sabbatical at Oxford (1996-1999). The honorable corrupted Claes was nominated Minister of State by the King of Belgium. Although only an honorable title and not paid for the job, the signal to the rest of the Belgian politicians was clear. They did not need to fear any effective prison sentence. In fact, the only painful measure was the obligation to return their booty to the treasury of the State of Belgium. Since 1990 a row of local politicians on the level of community, provincial and federal government have been subject to investigations concerning fraud, abuse of community funds and abuse of by the government issued VISA-cards. An example of abuse of government funds that speaks to the imagination is Minister of Defense of Belgium, Pieter de Crem. Visiting New York with his staff end November 2008 for a conference that was cancelled, his misbehavior attracted the attention of a Belgian female servant in a New York bar. Following his visit, bartender Nathalie Lubbe Bakker blogged their visit (in Dutch), talking about how disgusted she was of how drunk De

Crem was and how embarrassed she was about his behavior. Worst part, she wrote, was the fact that one of the politician's advisors admitted to her that the meetings they were there for on taxpayer's money were in fact canceled because the UN was meeting in Geneva. Couple of days later, someone from De Crem's office had a telephone call with Nathalie's boss, after which she was promptly fired. This was initially denied by the politician, and it remains unclear if her termination was a direct result of the call or the blog post in question. However, the trip was paid by Belgian tax-payers. Even though the meeting was canceled, he still decided to come to New York just because "he'd never visited the city anyway". Getting drunk in a bar is for a Belgian politician obviously business as usual and expresses the fact that he mentally stays in touch with his voters. Mr. De Crem is not to be blamed. His Belgian colleagues on every level of government made and still make traveling on public expenses and accompanied by wife to a national hobby. And the activity is considered to be fully acceptable. At least in the political environment it is. Another example of the bad model function of Belgium as 'Capital of Europe' is the Minister of Foreign Affairs, Mr. Karel de Gucht. Feeling the need to show the importance of Belgium during a visit to Congo, the former Belgian colony, he expressed in public his opinion that during his visit he had seen no good government. He talked as being a colonial inspector who has been there to see how the political development progressed. The president of Congo, Mr. Kabila, was rather embarrassed and the diplomatic relations between Belgium and Congo reached lowest point in years. Not guided by any diplomatic knowledge, Mr. de Gucht expressed in public his opinion that the Dutch Prime Minister, J.P. Balkenende, was a 'Harry Potter' with a grocer's mentality. Mr. Balkenende, after getting knowledge of the remark, obviously remembered that if one walks through a pig stable, one has to accept the odor and grunting of the animals and at first he did not react. After another Belgian politician of doubtable quality, Mrs. Vandenbossche, expressed her senses of malicious pleasure about the remarks of Mr. de Gucht, the Dutch government reacted slightly irritated in the way a psychiatrist reacts on the nasty remarks of his patient who lays on his couch. Mr. De Gucht also is, as his colleague Mr. De Clerck, a proponent of the separation of the constitutional powers, the Trias Politicas. After a ministerial meeting on which was decided to sell the Fortis Bank to a French banking group, Paribas, within a few hours his wife sold their shares of Fortis bank. A few hours after she sold them, they were worthless. His wife, a Belgian judge, denied any communication about the subject with her husband and during trial her colleague judged that there was no evidence that Mr. De Gucht had contacted his wife to tell her to sell those shares. Maybe an independent German, Dutch, English or Spanish interrogation team would have achieved another conclusion. And the anti-Mafia specialists of the famous Italian Carabinieri would certainly have been able to teach the concerned Belgian judge some lessons in successful interrogation and investigation methods. But Mr. De Gucht is right. The Trias Politicas is the basis of any functional democracy and in particular when it suits the man. And no man can be happier than him with a wife who is blessed with clairvoyance. Mr. De Gucht is a very strict man.

He is known for his honesty. In case of the accession procedure of Croatia to the EU, the Croatians hesitate to deliver a possible subject of war crimes, Ante Gotovina, to the Yugoslavia Tribunal (ICTY) in The Hague. In a reaction, Mr. De Gucht considered Croatia 'probably not ready' for membership of the EU. Someone could call that a way to put pressure on Croatia. Someone else would call it blackmail. If Croatia is economically ready for membership and it fits the political requirements of the EU, it should join. Otherwise it should wait until the conditions are achieved. The prosecutor of the ICTY is a Belgian. This fact may play a role in the remarks of Mr. De Gucht after his lobbying to get a Belgian on that post. A failure of the Belgian prosecutor of the ICTY would not exactly be an example of authority and Mr. De Gucht knows that. Mr. De Gucht is also very concerned about human rights everywhere in this world, as the Belgian government always has been. In 2003, the Belgian genocide law was legislated and it did not take more than one week before hundreds of complaints were lodged against US and Israeli politicians and military men. According to that law, a Belgian court was legitimated to prosecute anyone who committed genocide, irrespective of nationality of the offender or the location where the genocides took place. Unfortunately, during the same period the NATO had to decide about the location of the new headquarters. President Bush made clear that a possible arrest and prosecution of a brave military man, visiting HQ NATO and based on a Belgian law, was unacceptable. The decision to build the new NATO HQ in Brussels had to be reviewed under these conditions. The cast iron backbone of the Belgian political top, in particular Mr. Verhofstadt and Mr. de Gucht, turned out to be made of the material jelly-fishes are made of. The new law on war crimes was enfeebled immediately and offenders only prosecutable when the crime took place under full moon, with 3 white clouds visible from the Royal palace, a dove would, with its excrements, hit the right eye of the prime minister and the milkman stumbled over a banana skin. And that all had to happen at the same time. Obviously, economy is more important than genocide. From then on former President Bush, Mr. Rumsfeld, Mr. Cheney, Mr. Powel, Prof. Rice and many brave US military men were, when visiting Belgium, benevolent tolerated war criminals in change for the willingness of the US tax-payer to accept the financial burden of the presence of NATO Headquarters and SHAPE in Belgium. Mr. de Gucht is also very concerned about the future of Belgium and he wants, of course, only the best politicians, in particular liberals, to govern the country. And where can they be found elsewhere than within the family of very good straight forward and honest liberal politicians. The exceptional political gifted Mr. De Gucht is the proud father of a 24 years old son, Mr. Jean-Jacques de Gucht. Of course, a father is pleased when his child steps into his professional trail. And in view of the principles of Mr. de Gucht who are, like his back bone, as hard as cast iron. He fights as a lion to get his son on the place of the voters list where he belongs according to a proud father. And that is the top of that list. Carl Devos, a well respected political scientist in Belgium, described that as follows in an article in the Belgian newspaper Het Laatste Nieuws: Because the Flemish themselves also wish support, also political support, for their own sons and daughters, they apparently tolerate that the children of politicians get preference. This kind of clientelism is so much rooted in the Belgian political system that 10% of all politicians are son or daughter of a politician. A picture of Mr. Jean-Jacques de Gucht in Het Laatste Nieuws of April 15 2009 showed a young man who does not stand close enough to his razor blade in the morning and the local barber will not count him as one of his best clients. Fortunately, Mr. Jean-Jacques de Gucht has clear personal insights and in an article of the Belgian newspaper De Morgen of June 11th, stated that he feels being too young executing a post as minister in the Flemish parliament, if offered eventually. Seldom has a personal introspection of a would-be politician been a blessing for the population of a nation. Mr. Karel de Gucht was deeply worried by the fact that his beloved son suffered under the lack of any important job and found the solution. His son now occupies the job of spokesman on the subjects of public health and moral for the liberal party and the predecessor, a very principled man and medical doctor named Vankrunkelsven, left the political scene disappointed. In an interview in a Belgian newspaper, he bitterly mentioned that his successor was nothing but a schoolboy. Mr. Verhofstadt's remark some weeks before this extraordinary event, that the party top of the Belgian liberals had to be renewed and younger people had to take the places of the older, suddenly got a sinister character. But, as could be expected, the positions of the older party members like Mr. Verhofstadt, Mr. Karel de Gucht and Mr. Patrick Dewael were not subject of this vision.

Regularly, clouds of dust are thrown up in the center of Brussels. Cause is the vacancy in some international organization, preferable the chairmanship, Chief so-and-so or Secretary General. Belgian politicians of doubtable quality nervously run around to search for their Special Cooperation User Manual (SCUM). In Belgium, caused by the everlasting political controversy between French speaking Walloons and Dutch speaking Flemish, the SCUM is one of the most important written guidelines for dealing with all kind of problems between the two tribal groups of the political, financial, constitutional and law-and-order jungle that is called Belgium. Also in case of an application for chairmanship of the important Committee for the Promotion of Peaceful Co-existence between Frogs and Flies, the upcoming vacancy of High Representative of the EU for Foreign Affairs or the chairmanship of the European Committee, the SCUM gives the correct guidelines. It tells exactly whether the candidate has to be a Walloon or a member of the Flemish tribe, it weights the importance of the vacancy, the remuneration, the possibility to offer subordinate jobs to a row of tribe members, the opportunity to deal advantageously with lobbyists and last but not least whether the job includes a free daily lunch. After all plusses, minuses, comma's and periods are scrutinized, Mr. Karel de Gucht acts as illusionist, puts his high cylinder hat at the table and out of it comes the rescuer of Europe, Mr. Guy Verhofstadt. Depending on the importance of the vacancy the possible candidate also may be the local street sweeper or a young man who does not stand close enough to his razorblade and is only a bad customer of the local barber. The European Commission glances weary at it and compares the political situations of Belgium and Bulgaria. It decides that Bulgaria is, compared to Belgium, an example of a law-and-order nation.

These days, a phantom is reported to be seen in the middle of the night in the vicinity of several prisons in the neighbor countries of Belgium. This phantom checks main gates, height of prison walls, counts the bars in the windows and counts the empty cells. No one needs to worry about that weird phenomenon. It is not a phantom. It is Mr. De Clerck, Minister of Justice of Belgium. This same excellence is also seen during daytime in a strange procession, ahead of three thousand prisoners and trekking through Europe while searching for an opportunity to lock them in. Not strange in view of the fact that during the last 10 years the situation of the Belgian prisons has gone from worse to dramatic. Belgium has in total about 8.500 prison cells available while more than 11.000 inmates are behind bars. And in view of the fact that the famous Mr. Verhofstadt, being Prime Minister from 1999-2008 decided during his PM-ship that prison sentences of 3 years of less will not be served and the possibilities to condemn people to wear a CPS-bracelet is exhausted because of a lack of personnel and equipment to control the movements of this people, who strictly should also have served a prison sentence, much more prison cells should have been available. One could not blame Mr. De Clerck for not having enough prison capacity available. One could blame Mr. De Clerck for accepting the job as Minister of Justice knowing that he would not be capable of executing the job after the results of the perfect governmental period of Mr.Verhofstadt.

But Mr. De Clerck's conscience, being a lawyer, is elastic enough to accept that minor imperfection.

Mr. De Clerck shares the opinion of Mr. De Gucht about the independence of the three constitutional powers. But exceptions may occur. A Polish gipsy, named Adam G., killed in a Brussels railway station a young Belgian during the robbery of an MP3 player worth about 39 Euro. Adam G. flew to Poland and was shortly after arrested by Polish police men. Poland was willing to extradite the killer under the condition that he had to serve a possible prison sentence in Poland. The Belgian government accepted that condition. After trial and condemned to 20 years of prison sentence, the lawyer of the killer requested in a short lawsuit Adam G. not to be extradited to Poland because in a Polish prison he would, being a gipsy, possibly be maltreated by prison guards. In one breathe the total of the personnel of all Polish prisons and the Polish government were offended. The first for being gipsy crackers and the latter for being not capable of correcting the expected misbehavior of Polish prison personnel. An obscure Belgian judge decided thus, without having seen any proof of the statement of the lawyer. Mr. De Clerck expressed his opinion that another judge in an appeal court would correct the verdict. The fact that this Brussels judge took the word of a lawyer for the true without any evidence was for Mr. De Clerck no reason to have that judge send to a psychiatrist in order to check his mental capabilities. The Polish Minister of Justice, Mr. I. Dzialuk, was rather embarrassed and reacted with visible irritation. Mr. De Clerck mentioned the independence of the three constitutional powers not to intervene. His conviction and honesty in this matter was subject to doubts when Belgian judge Walter De Smedt, having to judge a notorious robber, decided to set the man free because two of his earlier sentences were not executed by Mr. De Clerks department. Reason: No place in Belgian prisons. Suddenly Mr. De Clerk forgot all about the independence of the three constitutional powers. He felt personally attacked by a judge who dared to point out that politicians should not dare to ignore the verdicts of Belgian judges. With bloodshed eyes, foam at the lips and growling sounds that had nothing to do with a respectable politician, Mr. de Clerk decided that Mr. De Smedt was a danger to the Belgian legal order. He totally forgot that Belgian judges suppose to be members of one of the three constitutional powers. By now Mr. De Smedt only may decide about cases of divorce in which both parties agree to that divorce and cases in which Belgian flies protest against being eaten by Belgian frogs. He will not be happy with his degradation and bitterly regrets figuratively slapping a politician in the face for not doing his job. And Mr. De Clerck is clearly not doing his job. At the end of June (22) 2009 he considered advanced release of prisoners against overpopulation in prisons. Protest against that intention made him show up with another proposal in June 24 2009. That was the release of prisoners because a hot summer was expected. The conscience of Mr. de Clerck seems to be extremely elastic. His strange behavior as Minister of Justice is not recent. Already in February 2009 his spokesman in a blog elucidated the confusing vision on the Trias Politicas of the honorable Mr. De Clerck. Another challenge for His Excellence was the case of attempted murder on a young Belgian, Mr. Wijffels, by two Ukrainian brothers. They were at the moment of the facts 15 and 16 years old. Their family had requested political asylum in Belgium. Although the legal action ran against juveniles, the family was definitively expelled meanwhile. The Ukrainians waited till the oldest son in December 2008 conditionally was released and then have left voluntarily. The brothers stayed after the facts respectively nine and fifteen months in a closed institution. They were been guilty to attempt murder, but a possible decision to place them in a closed institution for criminal non-adults could not be enforced because they stay in Israel. The senior of two is meanwhile no longer in an age to be eligible for treatment as non-adult and can't be placed. The Ghent Youth Court decided finally and at contumacy a reprimand for attempt to assassination. For Mr. De Clerck this weird decision was no reason to consider the concerned judge to be a danger to the Belgian legal order. The limits of lack of legal insight, monitoring of the legal procedures in Belgium, rejecting each responsibility for matters where the Minister of Justice for is sworn in and appointed, concerns ignoring him a letter with the proofs of failures by a local police unit, a Public Prosecutor and a female judge named Selleslagh of the Cantonal Court in Beauraing refusing pertinently to take knowledge of written proofs of extortion, tax evasion and black labor that were brought to their attention. The fact that one of the black laborers was also a municipality Council member of the local Liberal party may have played a role in her decision to act as an unguided judicial projectile and, with her verdict, let the extorter, black laborer and tax evader in the possession of the results of his crimes. Mr. De Clerck considered that to be normal behavior and did not put any efforts in restoring the Belgian legal order. Maybe his fear that no prison cells were available made him decide thus.

Under the excellent management of Mr. De Clerck resorts also the Belgian police. Mistakes, theft, crimes and fraud, committed by members of this organization, are seldom subject to prosecution. An interesting proof of the professional honesty of members of the Belgian police corps was the newly legislated fire weapons law. When the new weapon law in June 2006 was legislated, the ten province governing boards organized the possibility for owners of prohibited and illegal weapons to deliver them anonymously to the police, which many did. But instead of registering the submitted weapons on a list of fire weapons to be destroyed, some inspectors kept the most beautiful copies for themselves. They sold those to arms trafficking criminals, foragers and other illegal circuits. The most wanted copies were hand-made hunting weapons of the weapon masters of FN-factory that had values of up to 12.500 euro a piece.

The list of misbehavior, fraud, theft, counterfeiting, murder, police commissioners and judges who drive a car on public roads under the influence of alcohol and false warrants is that long that it seems to be normal behavior not worth punishment in Belgium.

Mr. De Clerck is a lucky man and in good company of loyal friends. Mr. De Gucht, the world-wide known Belgian who is allergic for bad government, Harry Potters and grocers and in the possession of a son who does not stand close enough to his razor blade to be well shaven and is a bad customer of the local barber shop, was willing to solve a delicate problem for Mr. De Clerck. Two secretaries of the Belgian Commissioner-general, Mr. Fernand Koekelberg, where obviously illegally promoted by the by then Minister of Home affairs De Wael. In a political environment as the Belgian is, this affair could easily be kept covered. Unless someone is getting troubles and knows about it. To get rid of the problem, Mr. De Gucht, in his quality of Minister of Foreign Affairs, offered Mr. Koekelberg a post as liaison officer on the seat of Europol in The Hague, Netherlands. Koekelberg refused, according to the Walloon newspaper La Libre Belgique, categorically.

The Gucht, by means of that golden side track, as a good informative source called it sneering, wanted to solve the problem of the Commissioner-general. Mr. De Wael denied any responsibility or wrong doing. Of course Mr. Koekelberg refused this golden side track. As a policeman he knew that policemen who are contaminated with the odor of any crime or irregularly are at best politely accepted by international colleagues but never trusted.

Mr. de Gucht is in the possession of a nose that smells unexpected financial possibilities. After the European elections, he resigned and kindly accepted the post of European Commissioner for Development and Humanitarian aid. The remuneration was good enough and, more important, a free daily lunch on public expenses was granted. And even more important: He could turn his back to the political, juridical and criminal mess that is called Belgium and deny any responsibility for being one of the three top politicians of the Flemish Liberal Party who caused this mess by ignoring the increasing problems during the eight years in which the savior of Europe, Mr. Guy Verhofstadt, acted asPrime Minister and of which Mr. Di Rupo, party leader of the Parti Socialiste said: "One snap of my fingers and he is gone."

Only for certain politicians of the different EU countries and the US this may cause some inconvenience. It is rumored that, after being forced by diplomatic politeness to shake hand with Mr. De Gucht, they inevitable have to go to the bathroom urgently. To wash their hands.

One could ask how the government of a country during many years could have the situation in their country financially, governing, juridical and political worsening without reacting. Maybe that question can be answered by a remark once made by a man who's nose for well paid jobs including free lunches, is well known in Belgium: Mr. Dehaene, former PM and predecessor of Mr. Verhofstadt. His remark was: "We solve a problem once it announces itself." He forgot to tell that the blind and the deaf never recognize a problem. Maybe that question also can be answered by the prevailing political mentality in Belgium. Maybe it also can be answered by the mentality of the whole of the population in Belgium.

The terrorist attack on New York, well known as 9-11, made the beloved Belgian PM, Mr. Verhofstadt, declare that Article 5 of the NATO Treaty did not apply. He was not the only one but for sure the loudest. Of course the brave Belgian government was loyal and willing to assist in military cooperation. The Belgian offer of four F-16 Falcon Fighters to protect US airspace caused a problem for the Pentagon. In the first place because the concerned US officers rolled over the floor by laughing and second: How could they fit these four planes into the already existing operations and an overfilled US airspace. But the offer was accepted and for some time the Belgians patrolled the blue American sky on places where they could not do any harm.

With the beginning of the war in Afghanistan, the Prime Minister of Belgium, the still famous Mr. Verhofstadt, in his different statements **never** stated that Belgium as a sovereign country was standing right behind the US. He stated that the European Union was standing behind the US. When he said 'we', he talked as temporary chairman of the EU. He never stated that the European Union was standing absolutely behind the US. As chairman of the EU he made immediately a statement that this 'standing behind' concerned the fight against terrorism. And after some days he enfeebled that 'standing behind' by stating that terrorist arrested in Europe would not be delivered to the US, because they might get condemned to capital punishment. And cooperation had to be negotiated, had to find a consensus within NATO and the EU, had to be thought over again etc. The Belgian worldwide known decision making process worked well and initially Belgium stayed out of any military operation. Except, of course, the inevitable humanitarian aid, plasters and now and then a flight with an aged C-130.

After the start of the war in Iraq, Mr. Verhofstadt opened his giant file system to find the right excuses not to cooperate with the US and GB in this important operation. The big piles of excuses fell out and an avalanche of the most ridicule reasons why Belgium should not be involved in any military operation covered the poor man. It took not long before the world started to condemn this war, condemn Pres. Bush and made PM Blair ridiculous. The terms 'war monger' and 'Bush' poodle' appeared to be common in Belgium. From then on in the Belgian newspaper appeared cartoons of the most disgusting kind about Pres. Bush, PM. Blair, security advisor Prof Rice and the top of the Staff of The white House. The Belgian Minister of Interior, Patrick De Wael made the top of the bill by a series of comparisons between Pres. Bush and a monkey. Later on explaining that some of his civil servants had set the series together and careless and without shame declaring that if Bush thought to be offended, he was willing to apologize. His behavior was that of a boy with an inferiority complex seeing someone being maltreated and after the offenders are gone kicking the on the ground lying victim. The facts were brought under attention of Pres. Bush, who took the same position as the Dutch PM Balkenende: Dealing with pigs means getting dirty feet. A very disgusting cartoon about Prof. Rice, being an impeccable lady and not contaminated with the smells of adultery and corruption as many Belgian politicians are, will only have caused an attack of serious nausea and, of course, after having a meeting with the Belgian Minister of Foreign Affairs, a painful hand washing with sulphuric acid and steel brush.

Again the question arises: Must the European Union be governed from a place in a country that:

1: has itself a government marked by politicians who are not capable enforcing the laws of the country?

2: wants the advantages of the presence of the EU commission on its soil but refusing to pay the costs of the international school, thus having the taxpayers of the other countries paying for it?

3: is condemned for the tenth time in 2009 for not complying with the obligation to put European directives into national laws? Over 2008 Belgium received seven condemnations for the same facts?

4: with knowledge and permission of the present PM, Mr. Van Rompuy, allows the present Minister of Finance Mr. Reynders to turn in a stability program with a budgetary planning for the coming years that was marked by the EU as: Incredible hypotheses, always sliding down budget objectives for the period 2008-2013, on-off interventions, no structural savings, missing information, no reforms, thus being the equivalent of a scribbling paper?

5: has a Minister of Finance who actively or by lack of political skills frustrates the fight against the tobacco fraud for which Belgium received 72 million Euros and had the money transferred to the national treasury?

6: abused for 9 million EU subsidies?

7: uses 2 obesities suffering politicians, Dehaene and Louis Michel, who considered the treasury of the EU, so the property of the people of the whole of the EU, to be their own gold mine and used funds for the modernization of the public broadcasting RTNC in Congo by the Belgian audiovisual facilities company Talent & Vision. In fact a pure commercial operation and only camouflaged as development aid. Coincidence or not, but the Belgian Minister for Development Aid, Charles Michel, is the son of Louis Michel, predecessor of Karel de Gucht, the present European Commissioner for Development and Humanitarian Aid.

8: is a capital of the criminals! Politicians and diplomats, who work in Brussels (Belgium), strike alarm: The city sinks in violence and criminality!

Another question that arises is, whether the people of Europe want to be governed by a European government that allows politicians of one of the less loyal countries to be prominent part of them, want a chairman of the European Council from that country.

Belgium is geographically not the center of Europe, is a source of an unreliable Court system with partially unreliable to corrupted judges and, according to the Belgian newspaper Het Laatste Nieuws, a Court of Cassation that covers doubtable judges as De Tandt, Selleslagh, Reynders (sister of the incapable Minister of Finance), De Lentdecker and Blondeel.

The bad situations in Belgium concerning justice, finance, police, corruption and criminality are developed and increased during the blessed period of government and guidance of Mr. Verhofstadt, being the puppet in the headstock theatre of his fabulous advisor Mr. Noel Slangen during eight years, Mr. De Gucht, proud father of a son who does not stand close enough to his razor blade and is only a bad customer of the local barber and Mr. Patrick De Wael being a man with a preference for monkeys and a fanatic supporter of the tactics of hyena's, i.c. hitting a man who is already down on the floor. And this all with the warm support of the majority of the Belgian politicians and continued by the famous former PM Mr. Leterme and his successor PM Mr. Van Rompuy.

This description of the Belgian government and its politicians shows exactly how the political moral in the EU developed during the last fifteen years. It was as contaminating as the black Plague in the Middle Ages in Europe and is common use by now. Every European politician is more or less affected.

Chapter 3
Donald Trump´s Europeans

The election of a new President in the United States is, every four years, in the whole of the world an event to be followed by almost every politician. Depending on the country of origin, the reactions in common are from very polite to very scornfully and everything in between. Except those from European politicians. European politicians clearly declare one of the candidates to be their favorite. This not being a prove of excellent insight in the thoughts of the American people, neither an expression of the desire to see the best man as President of the United States. Contrary to that. It could be compared with a person, suffering a serious inferiority complex and trying to cure it with a self palmed superiority complex. The usual result is an act of mud throwing at the undesired candidate.

During the election campaign of Donald Trump, the many European politicians surpassed themselves in the use of adjectives to describe him. They behaved thus as the keyboard terrorists on many Internet forums, who think they should express their dissatisfaction with certain situations in the most obscene way. Special to the brash statement "... and grab them at the pussy' was a common argument to prove Trump's incapability to be President of the United States. Would such an act indeed be evidence that the person is not suitable for the job of head of state, the heads of state of almost all countries in the world should be dismissed. Unless they are homosexual or asexual. After the subject was exhaustively used to put down Donald Trump as a pervert, a man who was sexually harassing women and the whole female sex relegated to sex objects, the attention was transferred to his mental capabilities, lack of experience in politics and lack of knowledge of how the political world functioned.

It is interesting to read the comments of some European politicians.

After being sworn in, Donald Trump has to keep in mind that his office forces him to meet with politicians of doubtful quality. Is it not their personal character, than it may be their way to execute office. But is he obligated to meet with people who offended him, made remarks about him that are only used in the social lowest parts of a society and permanently expressed the wish that he should not become the 45th President of the Unites States of America? Thus pretending that they knew better what was good for the US society than that society itself?

No true American may expect his President to meet them, shake hands with them or even mention them. With their remarks about their President, they are slapped in the face as well.

For a better understanding, we will have a look at those European politicians.

The first one in the row is the Luxembourgian Jean Claude Juncker, being the Chairman of the European Commission. His remarks are remarkable. And the answers to them as well.

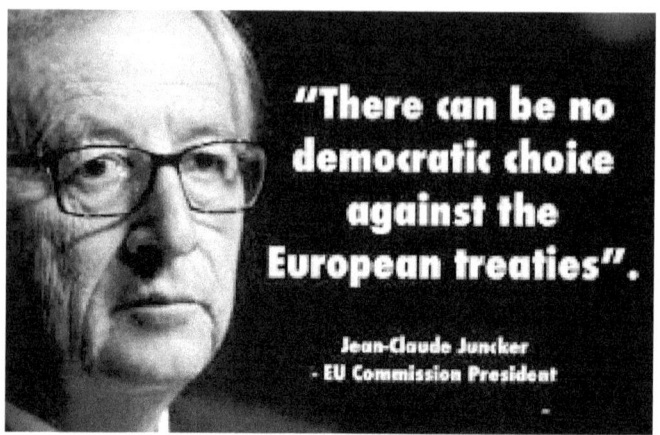

"There can be no democratic choice against the European treaties".

Jean-Claude Juncker
- EU Commission President

Source: geenstijl.nl

1: "Donald Trump's election has placed America's relationship with Europe at risk."

A.: That relation was: "The American taxpayers pay for our defense."

2: "Trump must be taught what Europe is and how it works".

A.: Juncker must be taught what the United States of America is and how its democracy works.

3: "The election of Trump poses the risk of upsetting intercontinental relations in their foundation and in their structure."

A.: Which will release the people of the United States of America from the burden of playing international police man and transfer that burden to the European Union?

4: "I think we will waste two years before Mr. Trump tours the world that he is completely unaware of."

A.: And, if he lacked any knowledge, will vomit permanently after coming back from that tour and will never set one foot outside the US again.

5: "He takes a view of refugees and non-white Americans which does not reflect European convictions and feelings."

A.: But reflects the convictions and feelings of the majority of average European of European origin.

6: "He doubted the cooperation within NATO and the way we organized our defense. That is rather malign."

A.: That cooperation ran as smooth as a bicycle with square wheels. And the way Europe organized its defense was basically leaving the burden to the tax payer of the United States of America.

7: "Mr. Trump's pledge to cut spending on NATO and his isolationist approach to foreign policy gives Europe no choice but to strengthen its common security and defense structures."

A.: Please do so. Bringing back the defense of Europe at the level of 1989, will exactly show how small the European contribution to that defense was. By now it is nothing.

8: "The Americans, to whom we owe much, will not ensure the security of the Europeans in the long term. We have to do this ourselves."

A.: You owe them the respect for their democratic choice to elect Trump and as for the European defense, just give it a try. The definition of an attempt is "striving without success".

9: 'We should consolidate the bridges we have been building across the Atlantic. Europeans trust that America, whose democratic ideals have always been a beacon of hope around the globe, will continue to invest in its partnerships with friends and allies, to help make our citizens and the people of the world more secure and more prosperous.

A.: That beacon has not yet been noticed by Juncker in view of his statement: The future of the European Union is too important to base it on democracy.

Some other statements of Juncker:

"I do not want to be a citizen of the United States and will resist if someone forces me to be."

"We decide something, let it rest and see what happens. If no one makes noise and no uprising breaks out because most people anyway do not understand what is decided, then we go again. Step by step, until there is no turning back."

Note by the author: What a nice and democratic thinking scatterbrain this Junker is.

The second European politician is Federal Chancellor Angela Merkel of the Federal Republic of Germany. She has her own opinion about Donald Trump.

Source: derspiegel.de

1: "Germany and America are connected by values of democracy, freedom, and respect for the law and the dignity of man, independent of origin, skin color, religion, gender, sexual orientation, or political views. I offer the next President of the United States close cooperation on the basis of these values."

A.: Since Germany is not really a democracy anymore, this would be a motivation for Donald Trump NOT to cooperate with Germany. (Every political group or organization in Germany disagreeing with Merkel´s policy is inevitable put down in the right or ultra-right corner or victim of prosecution).

2: "We don't always have a choice in whom you get to work with on the international stage."

A.: Donald Trump could have said it and then decide he HAS a choice.

3: "If I had known that my migration policy in the US election campaign Donald Trump played so much in the hands ... I would have decided otherwise"

A.: O dear. She would have kept all this raping, murdering and on the German society parasitical fugitives out of Germany. Only to have Clinton win the elections? Very principle.

4: "Only because of me, Trump has won the elections."

A.: So you were at fault. Japanese would commit Hara Kiri.

Since heads of state like Merkel are more or less restricted in expressing their opinion in cases like the elections in other countries, they very often leave that to other politicians as not to spoil future cooperation with the new elected head of state. So other German politicians were used to make Merkel´s point of view clear.

Sigmund Gabriel. Deputy of Merkel.

Source: theguardian.com

1: "Whether Donald Trump, Marine le Pen or Geert Wilders - all these right-wing populists are not only a threat to peace and social cohesion, but also to economic development."

A.: How about the disastrous policy of Merkel on migration?

2: "Let us wish that the candidate Trump remains a unique evil spook. Now it's a thumbs-up for Hillary Clinton".

A.: Meet the unique evil spook. If he allows you.

The German Minister of Foreign Affairs, Frank-Walter Steinmeier was, as his boss Merkel, convinced that Clinton would win the elections. Being in the position he has, he should have been a bit more careful in his way of expression. He was not and any contact came with remarks about Donald Trump that should make the latter feel forced to deny Steinmeier every personal contact. Maybe Steinmeier would have kept his opinion about Donald Trump behind his teeth when being blessed with clairvoyance and thus knowing that some months later he would be nominated to be the next President of Germany.

Source: rp-online.de

1: "Hate preacher."

A.: Said the hate preacher.

2:" When I think about an American President Trump, I am really afraid."

A.: Poor guy. Thinking about a German President Steinmeier, one becomes really afraid.

3: "What must worry us, among other things, is Trumps unpredictability. We cannot say what would be expected of a President Donald Trump."

A.: As mentioned. Steinmeier is not blessed with clairvoyance.

4: "Donald Trump will never be an American president, but he will provide valuable therapeutic services in a deeply neurotic country."

A.: Absolutely a lack of clairvoyance. But if Steinmeier means Germany with ´this deeply neurotic country ´, he may be right.

5: "The election result is different than most Germans would have wished for."

A.: He does not only lack the capability of clairvoyance. He also lacks knowledge about the opinion of the majority of the Germans.

6: "Look at the scripture called Donald Trump in America".

A.: For the United States of America: Probably yes.

Another European with a strong opinion about Donald Trump is the French President Hollande.

Source: telegraph.co.uk

1: "I find Donald Trump's "excesses" sickening."

A.: May I hope the sickness to be fatal?

2: "His excesses make you want to retch."

A.: Someone has a bucket available?

3: "Should the American people choose Trump, there will be consequences, because a US election is a global election."

A.: Indeed. This contrary to the elections in France. One of the consequences will be the ban on bad French wine and listeria- and salmonella contaminated cheeses in the United States.

4: "His slogans differ little from those of the extreme right in Europe and in France."

A.: His slogans differ little from those in Europe and France who resist the present political establishment that behaves like a slimy financial leech on their backs.

5: "The best service the Democrats can provide us with is Hillary Clinton to get elected."

A.: Another financial leech with her Clinton Foundation.

6: "Europe wishes to be together with the U.S. but has to be in a position to decide for itself, too."

A.: And Donald Trump has another vision on the subject and is in a position to decide for the United States.

Note by the author: Not even the French take Hollande serious.

A European politician who showed slightly disappointed about the victory of Donald Trump is the chairman of the Liberal group in the European Parliament, Guy Verhofstadt. An already discussed Belgian of questionable quality.

1: "One clown in Washington is as more as enough."

A.: Yes. So please visit Washington one time.

2: "The cronies of Putin and Trump are undermining Europe from within. Let's not allow this to happen. Let's fight back".

A: The cronies of Verhofstadt, De Gucht, Juncker, Schulz and many European parliamentarians are undermining Europe from within. Let´s not allow this to happen. Let´s fight back.

3: "Trump wants to take over her Majesty's role in appointing the British US Ambassador. Is that "taking back control"?

A.: No, it is not. It is a perfectly logical desire in relation to the future cooperation between the United States and the United Kingdom after Brexit has become final. Only fools don´t see that point of view.

4: "Europe is under threat. Only by building a stronger political union can we fight off the autocrats that surround us".

A: The only threats to Europe are Verhofstadt and his parasitic companions.

5: "Obama will be missed. Let's hope Trump can be convinced to work with EU & NATO to defend liberal democracy".
A.: On account of the US tax payer? Probably not.

A very special position on the election campaign of Donald trump has the political establishment in the Kingdom of The Netherlands. The head of state, King Willem-Alexander, never took position on the subject. He never takes position on any subject, which is, as he permanently states, Ministerial Responsibility. Thus honoring his new Royal Coat of Arms.

The Prime Minister, Mr. Rutte, known for his lies to the population on many subjects, could be called careful when expressing his preferences on who should be the new President of the United States of America. After Donald Trump's election, a sluice opened and would Mr. Rutte be a dog, the heels of Donald Trump would have been soaked by licking. He left his opinion to be expressed by several other Dutch politicians.

Source: liefdevoorholland.com

"I just have spoken with US President-elect Donald Trump. I look forward to the coming period to continue working together with Donald Trump for a safe and prosperous world and a strong relationship between the US and the EU. "

A.: Lick lick.

A Member of Parliament for the Labor Party, Mei Li Vos, saw this in a different way.

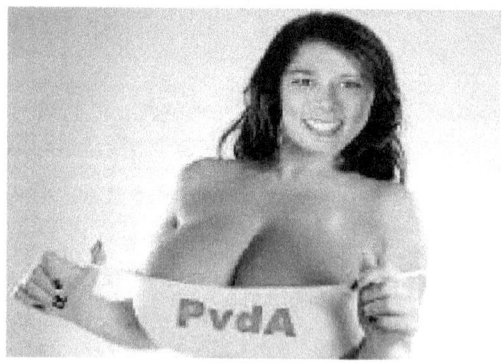

Source: dutch.faithfreedom.org

"After the message that Trump had won, I had a nightmare."

A.: Then dress better.

Party leader of the political party D66 (Democrats 66), Alexander Pechtold, also had some ideas. Out of his mouth came, like a long burp, the results of the performance of his labyrinthine mind. Incapable of recognizing the meaning of the word Democracy, he expressed the content of the dung hill that was hidden under his skull.

Source: de volkskrant.nl

1: "I consider Trump to be a rude and blunt peasant."

A.: Said the bubbling barrel of shit.

2: It is a terrible conclusion, but the message of division wins today. A man who from day one in his campaign insults people with disabilities, women, Latinos and all kinds of other people, wins today.

A.: Said the man who insults the Dutch people with his presence in Parliament.

3: "Populism again experiences a great victory."

A.: Said the populist.

4: "This is very, very bad news for the Netherlands and Europe. Trump has turned against NATO and Europe and does not want to give military support as did all previous presidents since the mid-twentieth century."

A.: The American tax payer will love it.

5: "Trump has, in his campaign, advocated a different course towards Russia."

A.: Maybe Trump understands the meaning of fruitful cooperation much better than all European politicians together.

6: "Economically this is a major setback. In the short term because of the increasing uncertainty in the world, in the long term because Trump turns emphatically against free trade and that goes very much against the interests of the Netherlands being Export Land."

A.: The latter being the main reason why Dutch politicians were in favor of the Clinton creeps.

7: "Dutch jobs and pensions can therefore come under pressure."

A.: Political liar. Those pensions are already from the moment of the use of the EURO under pressure, with the result that retired military men lost by now already 25% of their well deserved pension.

8: "Today I feel really bad by this result."

A.: When being forced to look at Dutch politicians and their boss, the king, me too.

Some other party members of the same party also thought to express their scatterbrained opinion.

Talitha Stam dug up some dung from under her skull:

"If Hillary does not win we are afraid of Trump. He is dangerous. "Not only for America, but also for our country and many other countries. "

D66 colleague Ilana Rooderkerk agreed with that nonsense, displaying clearly the lack of knowledge and qualifications of Pechtold´s female party members:

"He wants to leave NATO. He decides on declaring war or using nuclear weapons. We do not want him getting that responsibility. "

As for this nonsense: I am quite willing to teach these ladies the difficult NATO procedures, needed to obtain permission for the use of nuclear weapons on the European theatre. But they could have asked the Dutchman Mr. Jaap de Hoop Scheffer, former Secretary-general of the NATO, as well. He lives next door.

An interesting example of cowardice is Jesse Klaveren, MP for the party Groen links (Green Left)

Source: fubar.mobi

Before the elections took place, he called Donald Trump a mafklapper (it could be translated with rambling or indistinct)." He is the biggest mafklapper who walks around".

After the elections, and asked what he would say if meeting with Donald Trump, he answered: "He is a head of state now, so he will be treated as such".

The party leader of the Socialist Party, Emile Roemer, a type of second hand car dealer with guarantee to the next corner of the street, had a clear opinion about Donald Trump

Source: wanttoknow.nl

1: "He is dangerous for world politics."

A.: Fart one.

2: "He is a danger for the rest of the world."

A.: Fart two.

3: "Everybody is better than Trump."

A.: Fart three.

4: "Everything he says is a lie."

A.: Fart four.

5: "Everything he says is not feasible."

A.: Fart five

The party leader of the Labor Party gave some problems. Every time I tried to add a picture, I vomited spontaneously.

Asking others to do it for me, ended with the same result. I finally found a picture that suits the man and could add it without side effects.

Source: fubar.mobi

1: "Trump doing the craziest statements in recent weeks."

A.: According to the worst demagogue in the Netherlands.

2: "He seems to be a danger to the rest of the world."

A.: Said the man who seems to be the most dangerous man of the Netherlands.

3: "He did not give the impression that he is the man who can bring the divided America back together."

A.: Said the man who has split up the Netherlands with his parasitic behavior in favor of the EU.

4: "He is not the man who sees a role for America for a safer world."

A.: Is the opinion of the man who cooperated with other ruling parties to make the Netherlands the most unsafe country in Europe.

5: "I do not know if Trump is a man who carries statements after a long time. He himself would have problems with that."

A.: Said the man who does not recognize insults. Even if he stumbles over them.

Van Baalen is member of the European parliament, member of the Liberal fraction in that parliament and member of the Liberal Party of the Netherlands. He expresses his opinion about Donald Trump in the way his brain is capable to and in accordance with the real opinion of PM Rutte.

Source: hpdetijd.nl

1: "Donald Trump is, of course, impossible".

A.: For the Liberals in the Netherlands, of course.

2: "He is in no way reasonable."

A.: To warmongers.

3: "Trump throws NATO guarantees away as a friendly gesture to Putin."

A.: Build your own nukes on your own account.

4: "He always comes up with stories for which exists no solution".

A.: No brain to see one?

5: "But it is not impossible that he wins. Should he get it, then we will have to do business with his advisers."

A.: You very likely will do no business at all with whomever.

6: "With all that stuff in the world - IS, refugees, Russia - you need a strong American leader".

A.: So for the Liberals, refugees in Europe and Russia are just 'stuff'? We may presume the United States under leadership of Donald Trump is also just 'stuff'?

Han ten Broeke is another weird member of the Liberal Party in the Netherlands. He represents the party on foreign affairs and defense. As speaker for the party, he says what 'lick lick'-Rutte does not want to say.

Source: aquavit.wordpress.nl
"Let's all hope it will be Hillary."

A.: Shocking result, isn't it?

Before the elections took place and the many Dutch politicians indulged in a verbal orgy of dislike towards the person of Donald Trump, the Dutch government decided to give a clear indication of their preference for a particular candidate. The Clinton Foundation gave the correct purpose alibi and was surprised with a million EURO gift, given by a lady as weighty as possible, being Sharon Dijksma, State Secretary for Infrastructure and the Environment in the Cabinet of PM Rutte. Although sympathetic accepted by Mr. Bill Clinton, he did not really looked happy on the picture. Evil tongues claimed that he posed at gunpoint.

Source: Facebook

If I was going to quote from Dutch politicians about Donald Trump and would only mention the laudatory remarks, I was ready by writing the first line of this chapter. Would I mention all derogatory and outspoken insults of all politicians, I could go on for several weeks. For Donald Trump it would be enough to know that meeting Dutch politicians either leads to nausea or his heels get soaked by licking. Not a pleasant prospect. Thus the presence of a burly US Marine to guide politicians to the exit is a prerequisite for a healthy sleep.

Chapter 4
Trump and the NATO

Looking your worst enemy?
Kill your best friend.
  Old Chinese proverb

Yankees hurray.

In every town or village in Belgium and northern France, a small green corner with a couple of old conifers and yews, a few pillars with a black chain between them and a plaque are to be found. Even in villages with a hundred people, plaques with eight or ten names of young men who have given their lives to the concept of war, stand around. When the then President of the United States, Woodrow Wilson in 1916 decided that stupid Europeans with their perpetual belligerence had to be liberated, he staged a campaign that prepared young and innocent American male youth to be ready for a cozy stay in a coffin. One meter below ground level and with air holes in the chest or a ratty face and lungs from mustard gas. He talked about "the descendants of our common ancestors" and humanitarian duty to put an end to the war. With a little bit of luck, a boy still visiting secondary school, could remember that Denmark was the capital of Amsterdam and Brussels a quarter of Paris. Often, however, he could not remember anything about the geography of Europe, but was convinced to help his European brethren. The campaign was a success and Wilson was able to convince Congress that they " but needed to do". They did it in 1917 and the American troops landed in Europe and participated in the battle. 100.000 'Sammies' were killed and 200.000 wounded It was the turning point in the war and the Belgians could start with the creation of those little monuments after 1918 and Americans, leaving behind their dead young men, retreated to their country. The United States refused to join the League of Nations under the assumption that common sense would prevail in Europe now. The fact that League therefore never received any contents was just due to the fact that the United States did not join and did not want to intervene anymore in a part of the world that was constantly at loggerheads with itself.

In the current political leftist standards of this time, Wilson was no more than a vulgar warmonger who interfered with the internal affairs of Germany, Belgium and France, and risked the life of young Americans. We humbly stepped over it, but deep in our hearts we knew that he only did it because he knew there was a huge bubble of natural gas and oil, that would be found in the future near the cities of Slochteren and Schoonebeek. Little did he know that these towns were situated in the northern parts of the Netherlands and had nothing to do with the war. But never mind. He had to safeguard the future of the US oil supply. Didn't he?

However, the European countries did not do anything good with their obtained peace. During the interbellum period they were celebrating cheerful parties, robbed their colonies empty and cut their defense efforts to an absolute minimum because armies, who sit on their lazy buttocks, simply cost money. In 1939, Denmark even disbanded its armed forces to prove that it was a threat to no one. Tasty cheap it was, but in a room of the Reichskanzlerei in Berlin, Mr. Hitler, a fanatic follower of the famous Stratego game, rolled on the floor of laughing. He reportedly thereby also rolled over his secretary. But that must have been backbiting because Mr. Hitler was a well-known ascetic. He did not smoke, neither used alcohol. That, moreover, raises the question whether a second World War would have occurred had he used alcohol. In 1939, after a slightly tipsy Mr. Ribbentrop, the German Minister of Foreign affairs, had a warm chat with Mr. J. Stalin, a fatherly figure who possessed the ability to recognize work-shy elements at first glance to shove them off to forced labor camps, where they worked themselves to death (an estimated 30 million, which was statistics for him).

Mr. Hitler decided that there should be an end to the blatant colonial behavior of its neighbors. He decided to give them a lesson in colonial exploitation they would not easily forget. A shock went through all the neighbors and no one was actually prepared for the arrival of millions of German uniformed holidaymakers, who soon disturbed the streets in almost all European countries. The sluggish Belgian, the thrifty Dutchman and the wine boozing Frenchman suddenly realized it came to an end with their pleasant life. For a lot, by the way, literally. Especially the thrifty Dutch were hit quite unpleasantly. They were armed with guns M.96 (indeed, Model 1896), revolvers of the type Webley and Scott from the turn of the century and a collection of klewangs. The latter being a short infantry sword which name comes from the Dutch East Indies. Luckily they remembered that in some museums were still a lot of old cannons and at the gates of many barracks also the same models, serving as an ornament. It all went to the 'front'.

Mr. Hitler rolled back on the floor of laughing, had the inner city of Rotterdam changed by his air force and a few weeks later made some cheerful dance steps in the Bois de Compiegne in France.

The Americans once looked bleak at that idiotic Europeans and rightly decided that they had nothing to do with that mania. After all, you do not have to sacrifice your youth in favor of some murderous weirdoes. What they did was sending military supplies to their English relatives, which caused some annoyance in the Reichskanzlerei. There just happened to be a meeting with the Japanese ambassador, who had posed the question: "You declale the United States also the state of waal, Hell Fuhlel?"

At that moment the secretary came in and asked: "Mein Führer, do you want your sandwich with boar snout with sauerkraut in the nostrils?"

"Yes."

The Japanese Ambassador thanked the Führer sincerely for his solidarity with the country of the rising fireballs and left the room, while the secretary went to get the typical German delicacy with sauerkraut.

And suddenly the Europeans, and in particular a variety of foreign governments residing in London, remembered that those brave Americans came to help on a previous occasion. Alzheimer's disease did not exist. At that time it was simply referred to as dotes.

Congress listened to the call for help, turned it down and made the familiar gesture with the middle finger and pointed the president, F. D. Roosevelt, on his duties. It was not acceptable to sacrifice those young and promising Americans and let them waste time with squabbling in Europe. And they were right. But I have a dark brown presumption that some of those congressmen were clairvoyant and knew that a lot of hoodlums about twenty-five years later would hit the streets in Europe and declare the Americans to be rotten fish and rising banners with the title ´Yankee go home´. Still, it was fortunate for that ever mess-making European politicians that Hitler's secretary just at that particular moment had posed the question about sauerkraut and nostrils, because the Japanese grateful decided that 'Yes' to use and held on December 7, 1941 successful shooting exercises at Pearl Harbor.

This resulted in a rather furious reaction from President Roosevelt. The result of that furious reaction was that the raised middle fingers of the Congressmen went down and that Japanese Admiral Isoroku Yamamoto heaved the sigh: "I fear all *we have* done is to *awaken* a sleeping giant".

 Another result was that the Americans went to their sheds, searching for their knives and took that knives with the necessary other materials to convey it to the Pacific and the Atlantic. Had they trusted the capabilities of the clairvoyant congressmen, then they would have only attacked Japan and told Hitler: "Listen, mustache, because we say it once: "Recall your declaration of war and leave us alone. Otherwise we will put you at the bulky waste heap. "

I bet Mr. Hitler had accepted that offer. He had, after all, no need for a war with the United States. But then, of course, the Americans could not. They needed European oil. There was undoubtedly something of oil in the ground in Europe. And that's worth a few body bags. Right? Dirty imperialists!

But you can say whatever you want about those cowboys and movie stars: if they do something, it is done also completely. A good appeal was made to the deeper inner life of young Americans and the patriotic slogans such as: "Let's come to the aid of our European brethren", "the country needs you" and other nonsense and a nice picture of a thin man with a pointed beard and high hat, baptized as Uncle Sam, completed the call. All those young and misguided men thus went to war and ended the war with a festive fireworks display over the Japanese cities of Hiroshima and Nagasaki. The Japanese were so delighted by it, spontaneously about 80.000 came to be on fire and the radiating emotions overwhelmed about a same number of viewers later. The US estimate was that, had they to beat Japan in the traditional way, it would have cost the life of about 80,000 soldiers. For Europeans it did not matter. They finally only had to deal with those wretches who formed American free fertilizer for olive farmers in Sicily, dung in the Ardennes and beach decoration on the rocks in Normandy. For the Americans, it was something else. The costs of the paper for the letters that begin: "The President of the United States regrets to inform you that your grandson * son * father * (* delete as appropriate) died on the field of honor, etc... . . . „went up dramatically. Incidentally, the hero on paper always died quickly and painless. In that respect we can say that the Germans, as proponents of state promoted euthanasia, were ahead of their time.

After the war, the US-forces decided not again to go home, but first put things in order. That was necessary because wars ally Stalin begun to relay all sorts threatening language, and after a while it turned out that the Soviet Union was not better than the Third Reich. The Americans had by then become so immensely popular that many women threw themselves into the arms of the military Clark Cables, Fred Astaires, Gary Coopers, Rock Hudsons and Humphrey Bogarts, with which they laid the basis for the upcoming baby boom and popularizing The American Way Of Life. The flow of chocolate, cigarettes, liquor, nylons and parachute silk those fighting cowboys and movie stars also distributed was only side effect. Unhappy spouses of the ladies meanwhile looked wisely in a different direction and thus shared in the good gifts. The situation was understandable. They passed their liberator blood; Okay, a human gesture and that sort of things. But why did they not immediately supply the dollars to provide all their unknown descendants with early retirement schemes to be paid sixty years later?

In the euphoria of liberation, and after gratefully receive some billions of dollars from The Home of the Brave in the framework of the Marshall Plan, say just a financial helping hand for a set of political weirdoes who had not been willing to do what the Americans did, in one of those warped minds began to ring a bell and shortly after a number of politicians bellowed from their pulpit that Europe needed a defense organization. The basis for that organization, the West European Union (WEU) was laid in the Brussels Treaty of March 17, 1948 between Belgium, France, Luxembourg, the Netherlands and the United Kingdom. A real military alliance. Although the intentions were good, from the beginning on it looked like a denture.

General Dwight Eisenhower also was clairvoyant. Again one time crossing the Atlantic to hang in Nuremberg a set of politicians and war criminals? He gently pointed out that they already had a reasonable organization on the European continent which met all military requirements. And that was the SHAEF (Supreme Headquarters Allied Expeditionary Force), the Supreme Allied Headquarters of Eisenhower, in Paris. The Europeans saw the advantage, although England harbored some resentment against the presence on French territory. Actually a little bit too close to that long joker with his big nose, De Gaulle, who had insisted that the Americans had to fight to death on their way to Paris, providing him with the possibility to parade as first, ahead of the French brigade, into Paris. Our overseas movie stars, however, saw no problem there, and called for a European treaty that would oblige countries to assist each other in case of war. The European politicians once threw a shy glance at the east, still heard red bluster Stalin, looked once into the plundered treasuries of the individual states and warmly invited Americans to be part of that organization too. That was the third error of the founders of Uncle Sam. The first was the major crossing in 1917. The second was that they did not believe their prophetic congressmen and the third was a membership of NATO, as this organization was called. On 4 April 1949, with the signing of the North Atlantic Treaty, more popularly known as the Washington Treaty, NATO came to life. With that, the WEU, being a denture without teeth, was quietly relegated to a dark corner in some archive in Paris. Officially a headquarters was founded and staffed by each relieving sketch figures from politics of member countries.

The history of the NATO during about 50 years from its founding is marked by violations of the treaty by the European members on several subjects. Some interesting facts may help Donald Trump to decide whether to keep membership of the NATO or denounce the treaty:

1: With the exception of the United Kingdom and the United States, no member-country has obeyed the obligation to use 3% of gross national income for defense.

2: Although article 5 of the treaty says that an unprovoked attack on a member-country has to be considered to be an attack on the own territory, there never has been a European force situated on US territory in case the US was attacked from the west side. Not even symbolic. Neither has ever an Opplan existed to deploy European forces in the United States.

3: The objective of standardization for all material and equipment was never realized. Except with regard to the munitions, such as rifles (7.62 mm), the 155mm howitzer, and the 175 mm cannon (M-107) and necessarily the means of delivery of nuclear ammunition, such as 8 Inch howitzers, and Initially the Honest John artillery rocket and later the Lance. In general it can be said that the only thing that really was standardized, was the air in the tires of vehicles.

4: No NATO member has ever fulfilled his obligation to have stock for 30 days of warfare. Especially with regard to the precious 155 mm howitzer ammunition has no State ever had the necessary stock. Some examples: In 1980, the United States had 18 days of war stock, United Kingdom 14 days, Netherlands 12 days, Greece 9 days.

An incident:
In 1982, the Chief of the Logistics Readiness Center (LRC) of the War Headquarters at SHAPE was ordered to give a lecture to the national representatives at NATO headquarters in Brussels. This lecture was to cause the countries, especially with regard to the 155 mm howitzer ammunition, would stick to their commitments. Interesting to know that the Chief LRC, a Canadian colonel and righteous man, at the end of his speech concept wrote "that the money for it but had to be issued." I completed the lecture and gave it to a clerk to copy it for the representatives. But the last sentence was something to think over again. Shortly after I spoke to the colonel and, as his assistant, I pointed out that such designation would be not acceptable and certainly would lead to some critical and possible undiplomatic responses. I expressed my thought that national governments would not like to be corrected by any soldier whatsoever. After some hesitation the colonel decided to consult the Deputy Chief Logistics and Armaments. That interview lasted only some minutes and I could delete the last sentence in the lecture. Again I ordered the clerk to make 30 copies for the national representatives.

The day after the colonel took his copies and went to Brussels, gave the lecture and later that day came back embarrassed. He told me that, after the lecture, some representatives asked him what referred to the last sentence:

"that the money but had to be issued." Unfortunately, he took the wrong copies of the lecture to NATO HQ.

The representatives, and later their governments, were not happy with it and obviously had there been mutual exchanges, ending in the mindset and the belief that SHAPE, thereby SACEUR, did not have to concern themselves with the national policy for the national defense organizations.

Whatever diplomatic contacts have been exchanged after this incident, SACEUR Bernard W. Rogers decided the countries to point out their responsibilities with regard to their obligation regarding compulsory war stocks, with special reference to the related 155mm howitzer ammunition. He started with a visit to the Netherlands and spoke to the members of parliament. Before he had even left the country, the newspapers and news broadcasts were filled with negative articles and commentaries. I presume the visit to the Netherlands had been a try-out, because the SACEUR never went to another member-country to lecture them on the same subject.

In particular the leader of the labor party, Mr. Den Uyl (translated: The Owl) and nicknamed Shitting Bird, was furious about the cautious expressed remark that the Netherlands had entered into commitments which needed to be fulfilled. Not strange in view of the fact that Shitting Bird was allergic to everything that was American. Being a real socialist, he was one of the European visitors of the Russian party leader Brezhnev and was always present in Moscow on the first of May to celebrate the Labor Day, boasting the 'Internationale' on the Red Square with famous people like the party leaders of the Warsaw Pact countries.

5: None of the member-countries ever had the agreed numbers of ready combat units available. Again the Netherlands may serve as a sorrowful example. It supposed to have 1 Army Corps available and ready. That Corps consisted of 4 Divisions of 3 Brigades each. The designated defense line was at the northern border between the German democratic republic and the Federal Republic of Germany and 80 Kilometer long. In fact, only 2 Divisions (the First and Fourth) were standing Divisions. The Second and Third Division were to be mobilized. But of the two standing Divisions, thus six Brigades, only one Brigade was situated in Germany at barracks in Seedorf. The whole of the 1th Army Corps had to be in combat positions within six hours. An impossible military operation unless the military vehicles would have been built by Lamborghini and the roads to the defense line were empty. But in 1981 the ACE Medical Advisor at SHAPE conducted research on the reactions of the people during an eventual attack by the Warsaw Pact. The result of the research was that a large part of the population would clog the roads in their flight west to stay ahead of the attacking army. An estimated 25 million people would block those roads in western direction. Eventually, that people had to be shot off the roads to enable the Dutch forces to reach their defense lines. The agreed six hours could never been met. Besides, the two mobilization Divisions (Second and Third), would not be ready to be on their way within 36 hours.

But of course it was nice to have about 330.000 American cowboys and movie stars available to take the first hit from the enemy.

6: In view of the doctrine of Flexible response, that response could only take place after the Warsaw-Pact Forces had started their attack and were already on the territory of a NATO member. But that implied an early use of nuclear weapons on that territory. The procedure to get permission using a nuke was that the concerned country could deny permission. The force of the country that had to deliver the nuclear surprise was the second to choose whether to do it or not. The other members of the Nuclear Planning Group at NATO HQ only had a symbolic vote on the subject. The lack of sufficient 155mm Ammunition would led to an early use of nuclear weapons and although an enemy battalion is no doubt a wonderful target, it may be called disturbing when using a nuclear weapon, one also roasts all pigs in the nearby village, light in one time all cigarettes and have the milk boiling over in all pans at the same time. The Pentagon decided to change tactics and weapons and had the so-called ´neutron grenade´ developed. The grenade fitted the 155mm howitzer. The characteristics of a neutron grenade differ from the by then available tactical nuclear weapons. The 8 inch nuclear grenades and nuclear warheads of the Honest John cause most damage by their explosive force and heat development. The radiation is only a side effect. A neutron grenade has much less explosive force and less heat development, but the radiation is up to 20.000 R.A.D. Since 360 is deadly within three weeks, 20.000 R.A.D kills immediately. The purpose of the weapon was, of course, to kill the enemy in the tanks and armored vehicles. The fact that it left the vehicles undamaged was not important. But it left every infrastructure in the surroundings also undamaged and the people living there unharmed. The political members of the leftist Labor Party, including Shitting Bird and other political parties from the left wing spectrum, immediately called the neutron grenade a ´capitalist´ weapon because it killed people and left material undamaged. When then the Pentagon also wanted to introduce and stationed in the Netherlands, Belgium and Germany the Cruise Missile and Pershing II missile, Europe could witness a wave of protest of hundreds of thousands of people with the usual banners with the text "Yankee go Home", "war mongers" and other sweet cries. The by then Dutch Prime Minister, R. Lubbers, tried to calm the tempers running high and finally saw no other option than to formally reject the stationing of cruise missiles and the use of neutron grenades. He never attempted to explain to the people that the alternative was, to mobilize 2 Divisions and order the necessary conventional 155mm grenades to meet the requirements and fulfill the obligations to which the Netherlands had engaged itself. His behavior displayed the usual political cowardice the Dutch politicians are known for.

And, of course, it was nice to have about 330.000 American cowboys and movie stars available to take the first hit from the enemy eventually.

7: In 1990, a famous Syrian leader, Saddam Hussein, known for winning his last elections with 110% of the votes, ordered the invasion and occupation of neighboring Kuwait in early August 1990. Alarmed by these actions, fellow Arab powers such as Saudi Arabia and Egypt called on the United States and other Western nations to intervene. A coalition force under auspices of the UN and led by the United States started a sizeable deployment operation in Saudi Arabia to prevent Saddam Hussein from attacking that country as well. The operation was called "Desert Shield".

At SHAPE in Belgium the SACEUR, General Calvin, decided to the establishment of a special department that was called Crisis Response Group (CRG). The task of the group was coordinating logistics and communication. While still not operational, the many incoming documents and other means of communication were handled by Combat Management Branch of Operations Division. In September 1990, General Calvin feared a sudden attack by Iraq on Turkey and offered the deployment of the ACE (Allied Command Europe) Mobile Force. The Turkish government refused the offer. Partly due to the possibility that Hussein would regard this to be a provocation and partly because it considered itself capable of protecting its own borders. During the period September to December 1990, the threatening language of Saddam Hussein rose in intensity and directed against any country that would consider any aggression against Iraq. Although Turkey emphatically did not send additional troops to the border, the ridiculous threats expressed by Hussein became a reason to ask for the commitment of the AMF in December 1990. Belgium was requested by General Calvin to deploy their AMF component, a squadron F-16 Falcon Fighters. That turned out to be the wrong idea. To the then Prime Minister, Mr. Wilfried Martens, a good Christian who provided additional content to his faith by, beside his wife also having an affair with his no. 2 in the Christian People's Party, in between also divorced his wife to marry a young woman who then could share him with the no. 2, and finally got fed up with the situation and divorced him so that he, after all, married the no. 2, the question of General Calvin was a disturbing thought. In the first place because the Belgian F-16 Falcon Fighters were not equipped with an operational anti-SAM (Surface to Air Missiles) equipment, the so-called EWS (Electronic Warfare System). His first reaction was the statement that the Diyarbakir Airfield in Turkey was to be inspected to see if maintenance of the planes was possible. He could have had the answer from the chief of his military staff in one minute or calling SHAPE to get that answer from me after the time I needed to walk to the AMF section, find the last inspection report of the airfield, which altogether would have taken 5 minutes. Of course he could have taken a flight to Diyarbakir to execute the inspection himself. That would have taken one day doing it by F-16 or half a year if traveling by bike. It took him 11 days. His hesitations aroused anger within the SHAPE staff. Nobody understood why he hesitated.

A second request, now coming from the British government to deliver 155 mm howitzer ammunition, must have aroused real panic in the Belgian government and a blunt ´No´ was the result. The general negative mood towards Belgium changed into aversion and anger into loathing. Nobody understood why the request for ammunition was refused. Outside SHAPE and throughout Belgium the banners hanging around and the graffiti on viaducts, saying "Yankee go home", "War for oil" and other heartwarming twaddle were clearly visible and expressing the anti-American opinion of the habitants of the Land of the Drunks and the Home of the Psychopaths. But that opinion could not be a good reason to refuse the

71

request. Since the Warsaw Pact de facto did not exist anymore and many governments in Western Europe were already searching for possible buyers of their unnecessary heavy artillery and other equipment, no good reason existed to deny the British the possession of this ammunition. The cause was simple and first came to light after the end of Operation Desert Storm.

In Iraq, many foreigners, including Belgians, were employed in the oil industry. These foreigners were taken hostage by the Republican Guard of Saddam Hussein and situated around the places and facilities that undoubtedly were seen as military targets. Without informing his NATO allies, PM Martens sent a diplomat on a secret mission to Hussein personally to advocate the release of Belgians among the hostages. Of course that mission would not make sense to Saddam would Belgium provide the necessary ammunition to the enemies of Iraq. Fact is that the Belgian hostages were releases while hostages of other nationalities were still kept hostage. And forgotten were the 723.000 British soldiers, buried in Belgium as result of the liberation of Belgium in World War 1. Forgotten were the 114.000 US soldiers who died for the same cause and in the same war. Forgotten was even the slightest sense of loyalty towards the Belgian allies. It was an unheard case of betrayal.

8: When in 1991 the Yugoslavia War begun, the world watched the events in a disintegrating nation. The European Economical Community was the first political entity who tried to bring about peace in Yugoslavia, followed by the United Nations. During the beginning of the conflict between the ethnic groups, different plans and options were offered to end the conflict. None was really accepted and the war intensified with almost all population groups fought each other. Although NATO was in no way involved in that war, it was decided that there had to be set up at SHAPE two working groups. Those were the Working Group on Peace Keeping Operations and Working Group Peace Enforcing Operations.

Already from the beginning of hostilities in Yugoslavia France interfered in that war. Especially publicity. When it appeared that the US did not show the least willingness to engage in any way with the civil war by means the of the US Army, France called on the European countries to allow the operations in Yugoslavia under WEU flag under the auspices of the UN.

It will be clear that doing so was hoping for a situation where France, being one of the major WEU countries, could play the leading role and be able to refer to the unwillingness and inability of the US to do something about that war. The US reluctance is often widely reported in the French press.

The various mediators appointed by the UN were unable to bring the warring parties together. The role and influence of France proved even marginally (their soldiers even had to allow a Bosnian Minister, transported in a French armored vehicle and under protection of French soldiers, was killed by Serbs at a checkpoint in their armored vehicle and the Mitterrand visiting the besieged and shelled Sarajevo on the 28th of June 1992 was in the international press dismissed as a publicity stunt. What the Serbs learned especially in this period was that a marshmallow cannot exert pressure on anything and the UN was no more than a marshmallow. Especially the complex frameworks of accountability for certain things, such as the UN for negotiations, the WEU for the troops and military operations, which then had to be led by NATO since the WEU had barely facilities and UN again for relief and food supplies who were to be protected by WEU forces which were to be withdrawn from NATO, gave a picture of stupid political and military degeneration which made the Serbs screaming of laughter roll on the ground. Led by France, the European countries called increasingly to the interference of the US and French media suggested meanwhile that the US only fought wars and easy only if their oil supply was being compromised.

This view was soon adopted by other European media. However, the fact that the US formally refused to set ground troops available deprived France of the possibility to put the US into a position in which it could blame itself. In May 1994 Mitterrand got that opportunity. Flights carrying relief supplies, which were carried out by the USAF over Muslim areas, were also used to drop weapons. This news appeared one time in one newspaper in the Netherlands and was apparently censored by the government. The French had a legitimate interest in this American activity became well known. It would outrage the European partners, who were active in Yugoslavia, because the Serbs could accuse NATO of being not neutral in the conflict and consider NATO forces in Yugoslavia to be enemies. The affair could cause a controversy between the US and the EU-group within NATO, as Mitterrand wanted.

An incident:

On June 6, 1994 a sergeant-major was on duty as staff assistant in the Defense Crisis Control Centre of the Ministry of Defense in The Hague. With the usual accuracy he followed all the news from European TV channels of which he understood the language. It was an older man with a long experience of working in the international staff of SHAPE and an even longer experience of working with Americans at all levels and in many functions. He was absolutely loyal to his country and regarded NATO as the only guarantee for freedom. A soldier of the communications cell came in and handed him a stack of incoming messages. He leafed through it and saw the usual amount of messages from many deployed units. Then his eyes fell on a copy of a notice of the Ministry of Foreign Affairs. Het document was classified as secret and marked Wijnandts 169. Initially he read it quickly, and then the implication of the text dawned on him. It was a statement of the Dutch ambassador in Paris, who declared that he was informally and amicably approached by the French Chief of Defense Staff, who had told him that the US Air Force, simultaneously with the dropping of food by Serbs trapped Bosnians in Yugoslavia, also threw off weapons and ammunition. The sergeant-major knew that, would this message also reached other governments involved in the war, a conflict between the US and the Euro group within NATO would be unavoidable. And that seemed to be the purpose of this message. The sergeant-major also was well aware that the by then Minister of Defense maintained the same opinion about the US as the French Mitterrand did and likely would not react until he got the opinion of his European colleagues on the subject eventually. He looked at the clock and saw it to be 20.00 hours. It was time for the news broadcast. He switched the TV-channel to the Dutch broadcast and watched the, mainly local, news. Then a reporter appeared and reported about the visit of the President of the United States to France in conjunction with the commemoration of D-Day on June 6, 1944. On the TV-screen appeared Bill Clinton with Mitterrand, walking over the American cemetery of Colleville-sur-Mer, the latter backslapping Clinton and stating that the French people was eternally grateful for the sacrifices of all this young Americans, who sacrificed their life for the freedom of France. The sergeant-major took the Wijnandts 169 message from the pile. Looked at the text again and saw it dated 6 June 1994. Then he looked again at the TV-screen. The gesture of Mitterrand gave new meaning to the concept of betrayal. That long night of duty, the military was torn between loyalty to his country and to his understanding of alliance. Then he made up his mind. The message only would have impact when it was send to the other European nations too. Was it, then at least one of them would inform the US anyway. If not, he had to do it. He picked up the phone and called a number.

Seven days later he was interrogated by the counter intelligence service. The final result was a transfer to a unit where even the inscription on the packaging of sugar in the cafeteria was already too high classified. They understood the reasons why he relayed the information to the US and decided that he had not been able to make the transition from international work to a national task. Had he been clairvoyant, he would have known that Clinton one year later would betray a few hundred of his comrades in Srebrenica by denying air support for Dutchbat in favor of French and British hostages in Yugoslavia, held by the Serbs. During one of the days after his transfer, a Dutch newspaper reported that Clinton, during an interview, expressed his dismay about the loyalty and reliability of the French and two week later two US diplomats in Paris were declared Personae non Grata and expelled from French territory.

Chapter 5

Trump and the ISLAM

During the sixties, many European countries allowed so-called guest laborers, mainly from Morocco, Turkey, Algeria and Tunisia, to work in European countries. Being Muslims in predominantly Christian countries, they hardly were willing to adapt to the local culture and kept a low profile. Mosques were not present and the locals barely took note of the presence of Muslims. They were expected to leave the country again after some time. They did not. Contrary to that, many of them requested family reunification using the existing legislation. It happened in almost all countries from Sweden to Italy and in between. Many of them, after being resident for five years, requested the nationality of the country where they lived and acquired it. They soon discovered that, being fired and living for some time on unemployment payment, they were eligible for social assistance. Since that was close to minimum wage in many countries, they hardly found reason trying to find another job. That situation was quickly relayed to relatives and acquaintances in the homeland and the European countries saw an increased number of people from the North African countries coming as guest laborer, political fugitive or within the framework of family reunification. During the seventies and eighties, added to it were the fugitives who claimed political asylum based on persecution on grounds of religion, political opinion or sexual orientation. Many of them rather quickly got the so-called status A, which gave them permission to apply for work, a house and the coveted social assistance as long as they found no job. Most of them were

Muslims. They were not interested in integration or assimilation and tried as much as possible living together in the neighborhoods of the larger cities. For the indigenous population, living in those neighborhoods was impossible by harassment on the part of Muslims. Many moved to places where no Muslims lived and the empty houses soon were hired by Muslims. Residents, who had a house in possession in those neighborhoods, were forced to sell their homes at prices far below the value. Even those houses were soon in possession of Muslims. As a good example, the town Borgerhout in Belgium may serve. Already in the nineties it was generally referred to as Borgerocco since mainly Moroccans resided there. From the nineties, the phenomenon of Muslim neighborhoods in almost all major cities spread throughout Europe. The continuation of this process was the call for mosques throughout Europe. Some countries, like Germany, had a so-called church tax whose proceeds were distributed among the various religious movements. Under that legislation, coupled with legislation that guaranteed the freedom of religion, mosques were built. In the countries where the church tax did not exist, the funds for the construction of mosques came from countries where Islam was the state religion. This proved to be an uncontrollable phenomenon which the governments of the countries concerned closed their eyes for during an extended period. Because not enough Muslim clerics in European countries were available, soon came a demand for mullahs to fill those posts in the mosques. These Mullahs all came from Morocco and Turkey. They did not speak or were willing to learn the language of the host country and soon was discovered that many of them preached their religion in such a way that it could be called hate preaches.

Muslim districts in big cities.

In almost all major cities in Europe arose larger districts where only Muslims lived. And thus appeared phenomena that were typical of Islam. The respective Governments were no longer able to enforce the law and many aspects of the Sharia, the Islamite legislation, were introduced. Muslim districts became no-go zones, were the police and any other form of authority were refused. In cities such as Brussels, Berlin and in English cities pre-emergency calls were made to the police, who had to experience that their patrols were ambushed. It often resulted in wrecked police cars and after a number of cases, there was no police or any other form of authority anymore. That cleared the way for the influx of illegal Muslim migrants. Although the districts were hardly or not accessible to non-Muslims, the other parts of the big cities though for Muslims were, which caused a large increase in crime. This situation grew strongly during the first decade of the 21st century. It marked the end of the period when Muslims were only a small minority and arranged with low-profile existence in a predominantly Christian and Western modern lifestyle.

Sharia ruled districts.

It is well known that, according to the Sharia, Muslim women may not marry non-Muslims. Muslims cannot give up their faith or convert to Christianity. This means automatically that Muslims cannot mingle with the population of countries to which they emigrated. In many European countries this led to tragic incidents in which Muslim girls, who were in some way linked to a non-Muslim friend and in an often appalling way were killed. Sometimes this was made public in newspapers that usually did not belong to the mainstream media. In government circles this incidents always were called isolated events that had nothing do with Islam. But in Muslim circles they were called honor killings. Although first degree murder, none of the perpetrators if ever arrested were given long prison sentences. One may wonder how many in Europe illegally living young women have been victims of honor killings. It must even for the dumbest politician be clear that Muslim enclaves in big cities also form the base for Muslims who believe the Koran to be taken literally and thus raids on Christians may be performed, after which they return to safe Muslim port. No Muslim father, no Muslim mother and no Mullah will ever tell him or her that the law of the country in which they reside must be respected. According to the Qur'an, Muslims owe no honesty or loyalty to Christians. But the most unpleasant thought about these Muslim districts is, that they still extend, the habitants become more violent during riots and, many of them living on social security, become more demanding.

Muslims in political parties.

In the seventies, especially in the Netherlands, political parties were faced with candidates, who came mainly from Morocco and Turkey, for membership of the party. It was not long before almost every party did have a foreigner on the list for membership of parliament. They were scornfully called 'Alibi Ali's'. For the concerned parties, it was a proof of tolerance and understanding for the ´new´ countrymen. Because the candidates had two nationalities, many wondered to which of the two countries of which they were nationals, they were loyal to. Initially it seemed to be no problem, and especially those parties who had many Muslims on the list of candidates for parliament, made great gains in the elections. This due to the fact that almost all immigrants voted for their countrymen. The Labor Party was the biggest winner with this tactic and in the cities of Amsterdam and Rotterdam one soon saw more civil servants of foreign origin than proportionally was justified. No one cared. But the number of cases of corruption increased and the number of unjustified or based on vague data allocated grants to Muslim organizations also. In 2015 was discovered a loss of 56 million in the city budget of Amsterdam for which no single agency could give any explanation. Eventually, they could do nothing but accept the loss. Finally, a member of the D'66 party stated that one should not attempt to trace that amount because it would still remain untraceable. In the city of Rotterdam, the Labor Party received so many votes that electing a Muslim mayor made perfect sense. However, this also means that Rotterdam has a very large Muslim minority that will grow relatively quickly to a majority. If that is the case, the skyline of the city will soon be dominated by minarets of mosques. And one wonders how long it takes before the many municipal regulations will be adjusted to the Sharia.

Two passports. Two nationalities.

Many countries from were immigrants in Europe came from, do not allow their citizen to give up their former nationality. Since none of the countries in Europe have legislation that prevents in this case the person to get the nationality of the country where he lives, after five years he or she is eligible to apply for nationality of the country of residence. The result throughout Europe is that of millions of people have two nationalities. Their isolated living conditions and their refusal to integrate or assimilate into the population, make a check on their income virtually impossible and even their whereabouts are often uncontrollable. Since many live on social security, which is, for example in the Netherland about € 1.100 monthly, it is perfect possible to go back to Morocco where the average wage is about € 300 monthly on which one can live reasonable comfortable, many Moroccans indeed live in Morocco to return regularly to the Netherlands because they need to prove that they are living in the Netherlands. The Dutch government does not seem willing to have these cases of, in fact fraud, investigated. The governments of Morocco and Turkey are not eager to provide documents about the income their citizen have in the homeland. Would a Turk or Moroccan also work in his homeland, he would lose his social security payments in the Netherlands. Since Muslims are not obligated to honesty to non-believers, false official statements and documents can be delivered without shame. Even if concerning the amount of children. A Turk or Moroccan having children in his homeland, making him eligible for child benefits. They range from € 200 to almost € 300 quarterly. Even if the government would not be willing to give fraudulent documents stating that a man has four or five children in the homeland, bribery of an official is easily made.

Refugees

From the beginning of the war in Syria a flow of refugees came to Europe in all kind of ships, small boats and even rubber boats trying to reach the European mainland from the coast of Libya or via the route through Turkey, Greece and

Bulgaria. What begun with desperate people escaping the horror of the regime of the Islamite state in Syria, ended with an orchestrated exodus of mainly male fugitives in an age that presumed capability to resist the Islamic terror. The northern European countries accepted altogether millions of refugees of which many disappeared into the already existing Muslim districts in the big cities, knowing that their application for the status of official recognized fugitive would be denied. Those who were, usually did not try to obtain a job. The lack of knowledge of the local language and because of that, the them offered low quality jobs, were not paid well enough to make work attractive. The difference between a social payment and a minimum wage is so little that hardly anyone even tries to give it a change. This resulted in crowds of rather young men with no activities to keep them busy and that slowly fell into crimes such as sexual assault of women.

Being Muslims, the Friday prayers they attended and listening to the hate preaches of the many fundamentalist Mullahs resulted in excesses with an aggressive faith practice was becoming more common and resulted in the blocking of streets where prayer exercises were held. They appealed to the law which guarantees freedom of religion. Already from the beginning of the mass immigration, and perhaps because of it, the in the country born young Muslims began to manifest themselves strongly as Muslims. They harassed people in the street for no reason and committed crimes such as robbery, assault and vandalism. From 2012, one could conclude that the authorities in the various countries put newspapers under pressure to no longer report these activities in the newspapers. They wanted to prevent the resistance of the local population against mass immigration in general, and the risen aversion against Islam. Organizations, who opposed the arrival of so many refugees, were designated by the governments of the countries and the mostly leftist political parties as extreme right or Nazis. Especially during the year 2016 increasingly symbols of Christianity were victim of vandalism. The number of cases of sexual assault rose and even led to mass assaults, involving large groups of Muslims isolating women and abused them in public places. Even those cases were dismissed by authorities as incidents. The number of cases of Muslim women wearing a burqa in public and demonstrated for the right to wear them, rose. By now, 31 December 2016, all heads of states in Europe have addressed their population in Christmas messages. Inevitable they all called to be tolerant to each other and respect each other's culture, customs and religions. An empty call because the peoples of Europe were already centuries tolerant. The speech of the King of the Netherlands was full of generalities and reached the top of the bill. Quotes: ,, Anger cannot be the end," he assured, citing the violence in Syria, the refugees and the recent attack on a traditional Christmas market in Berlin. "Several populations are more hostile and extreme to each other. An open discussion is often impossible, "observed the king. ,, Can we solve peacefully any problems? The violence can often come close." ,, We so much would like to know ourselves being secure. But there is so much that makes us worried. Extreme seems to be the new normal " More than ever, he focused on the Christian values of mutual understanding and acceptance in the belief that everyone is equally valuable: "We want to live here: as free and equal people."

This nonsense was spoken by a head of state who´s hallmark is denying any responsibility for whatever the Dutch government does and decides to. And this to the disadvantage of many millions of Dutchmen. No wonder the reactions on this speech on Facebook came quickly: "That king´s message about tolerance better can be focused, in Arabic, on aggressive Muslim youngsters, Muslim scum , mullahs who have nothing but hate sermons, Christmas tree destroyers, burqa wearers and his important oil friend, the King of Saudi Arabia. We were tolerant, and had a tolerant society for centuries and willing to take in the outcasts from elsewhere. Just ask the Pilgrim Fathers, the remaining Spanish soldiers from the 80-year war, the Huguenots, Jews and many other groups. This king should again care about his own people. And those are the many homeless, the elderly driven into poverty, the on medical care dependent elderly, the by the government robbed pensioners. Then he can equally interfere with a set of political grabbers in the treasury. King: Just enforce compliance with Dutch laws."

One could say that, reading the content of many Christmas speeches, one is only tolerant if sacrifices one's own culture, customs and religion in favor of the Islam.

At present (31 December 2016) Europe is in the grip of fear for street violence, rape, murder, crime and the threat of terrorist attacks by refugees. Would all this Muslim refugees have arrived with arms, they would have been stopped with military violence at the outside borders of the European Union. They arrived unarmed. And the arms were sent separately. By now the whole of the European Union has many more violence prepared refugees than there are active serving soldiers and policemen.

President Donald Trump and the whole of the United States will face the same problems within years. The only difference between the situations in Europe and that in the United States is, that almost no civilian has firearms while in the US almost every citizen may have them.

Chapter 6
THE IMPACT OF LETTERS

Heads of states are usually surrounded by vast staffs, preventing ordinary citizen to approach him or her and thus avoiding him or her getting knowledge of sometimes and maybe even often, information that would make him change his or her mind on certain subjects. Rarely a staff member takes the time to read letters, Emails or other means of communication and decides to dig into the subject and bring it to the attention of his boss.

The following message to the staff of PM Tony Blair of the United Kingdom was such a message and found the right staff member.

Mr. Verhofstadt, an in this book well described individual, thought to be the perfect candidate for a political job, every politician is dreaming of. And that was becoming President of the European Commission in 2004. For an obscure Belgian politician with the typical background of politicians who promise golden mountains and bulls with golden horns, to forget his election promises as soon as he is elected, a job that would complete his creepy political career in the Belgian political environment with its corruption cases and would signify his way of executing politics to be the only right one. Nominated as candidate for the job, he thought it to be granted in advance. That was the wrong idea. Mr. Tony Blair, by then Prime Minister of the United Kingdom, had other ideas about the qualifications a successful candidate had to posses. Since he once clashed with Verhofstadt during an earlier confrontation, he vetoed the nomination of Verhofstadt. This interesting affair attracted my attention. Living in Belgium and following the events with pleasure and cordially supporting Mr. Blair´s veto, on the 27th of May 2004, I was reading a Belgian newspaper. One of the articles taught me that Mr. Blair withdrew his veto against Verhofstadt after the man visited the British Prime Minister for a personal interview in which he asked Mr. Blair to withdraw his objection to the nomination. A quick action was required and thanks to Mr. Bill Gates and his Microsoft, Google and a quick search on Internet I found the website of Downing Street nr. 10. On that website was the usual internal Email form to be found. I completed the personal questions on the form and wrote the following message:

Dear Mr. Blair,
To my dismay this afternoon I had to read in a Belgian newspaper that you have withdrawn your objection to the nomination of the Belgian Prime Minister Guy Verhofstadt for the honorable task of President of the European Commission. I fear that the appointment of Verhofstadt or any other Belgian politician, to this position is an insult to the British people, the British Government and you personally. Therefore I would like to bring some facts to your attention:
1: In December 1990 the then Belgian Prime Minister Martens initially refused to make available the Belgian component of the AMF, which is a squadron of F-16s, in favor of the deployment in Turkey during Operation Desert Shield,

previous to the Operation Desert Storm. Only after indignant insistence from the side of SACEUR, he decided to give the Belgian AMF-component available. The decision took him 11 days.

2: In the same period, prior to the Operation Desert Storm, the British Ministry of Defense requested the Belgian government to deliver 155mm howitzer ammunition. The request was denied without any reason. After the war, the reason turned out to be the following: Before Operation Desert Storm, the Republican Guard of Saddam Hussein took hostage many of the foreigners who were working in the oil industry in Iraq. Those hostages were placed everywhere around objects of which the Republican Guard assumed that to be military targets. Prime Minister Martens sent on a secret mission a diplomat to Saddam Hussein with the request to release the Belgian hostages. Would that diplomat have asked for the release of all foreigners, then Hussein would probably have refused. The Belgians were released. Under these circumstances, Belgium clearly could not provide ammunition to one of the countries participating in Operation Desert Storm. The incident was in the news because the diplomat apparently wanted to make his glorious role in rescuing the hostages known in Belgium

3: Before and during Gulf War II, The UK was ridiculously criticized in the Belgian newspapers while you personally were insulted as 'Bush` poodle'. He could have called US President Roosevelt in WW2 ´Churchill´s poodle´.

4: During and after Gulf War II, you as well as American politicians and military men were accused to be war criminals and Belgian newspapers and politicians insisted on prosecuting you and American politicians and military because no weapons of mass destruction were found. Such while after the Persian Gulf War, the United Nations located and destroyed large quantities of Iraqi chemical weapons and related equipment and materials throughout the early 1990s, with varying degrees of Iraqi cooperation and obstruction. The 1999 disarmament report by UNSCOM listed large quantities of WMD material that was unaccounted for. Verhofstadt, as Premier, should have known that because one of the members of the UN team, searching and destroying chemical weapons in Iraq, was a Belgian scientist. He nevertheless allowed his fellow politicians to criticize and in a very derogatory manner had their opinion published in the newspapers. You may be aware of the fact that in the management of many Belgian newspapers often a politician, failure or active, has a post as 'advisor' for the newspaper and follows the opinion of the government.

Accepting Verhofstadt as European Commission President is like getting a slap in the face, and then in response say thank you.

I hope this message will reach you in the proper way and I sincerely hope that you come back on your decision to drop your veto against this man.

Sincerely yours,

C. Brouwer

WO1 RNLA (retired)

Already the next day I had the pleasure to read that Mr. Blair changed his mind again and vetoed the nomination of Mr. Verhofstadt.

Not all letters, even written with the best intention and based on a military career that justifies writing them, find their way to the right staff member of a head of state or is intentionally blocked by some authority. The following was blocked by the US Ambassador in Brussels.

This letter could have been the model for the election program of Donald Trump. Many of his election promises and plans are found back in it. Unfortunately, written 16 years too early.

C. Brouwer
Belgium
20 October 2001

To: The President of the United States of America
    The White House, Washington
    United States of America

Dear Mister President,

With this letter I might kick open doors that are already open. But maybe there is one still locked and in that case you might not like the contents of the room.

After the attack on New York and the Pentagon you have expressed the opinion that, starting a war against terrorism, it is not a war against the Islam. This is far beside the real facts. It **is** a war against the Islam. Terrorism is a wide spread phenomena and not restricted to Muslims. That is true. But what after having finished the Taliban as a protector of Bin Laden? Will you continue your long battle against the IRA or the ETA or the Marxist revolutionary groups in South America? I don't believe that. If you really want any success in your battle against terrorism, you have to continue against other Muslim terrorists IN Muslim countries. This means that every Muslim in this world will consider you to be a liar, because only Muslim countries are "victims" of US aggression. At this very moment the Anthrax virus is exported to the US. It needs some industrial capability to produce it and the distribution of it is at the moment rather difficult because of the measures that are taken in the US. But how about of a fool of a Muslim doctor in Africa who breeds the EBOLA virus and exports it to the US as a food product like coconut milk or any other usually exported product. The time of incubation would allow the sickness to spread in such a way that the US would have an epidemic that would be really disastrous. And you could never find the originator of it. And this scenario counts for many other typical African and Asian diseases as well.

Transport of all kinds of dangerous products is an intensive affair in the US. You cannot stop that without destroying the US economy. But the initiative of one Muslim driver of a 20 tons LPG truck could make more victims than those of the 11th of September. I could do it with 250 gram desensitized pentrite, an electric igniter, a battery and a remote control devise of a toy without knowledge of the driver. And I would not have to sacrifice myself.

This letter is not supposed to be a lesson in terrorism but, Mr. President, be sure that there are much more ways to commit acts of terrorism than I could write down in one day. Only the fact that terrorists have not much fantasy saves the US for the worst. They think in knives, rifles and explosives, generally in fear caused by violence.

But be sure that with every attack on a Muslim country or on Muslims, more individuals will come to the idea that they can acquire eternal holiness by killing Americans in one way or the other. That does not mean that you should stop your war at the moment. Contrary to that indeed. But a new view on the future of the role of the US in this world is inevitable.

THE VISION OF THE ISLAM ON THE WESTERN WORLD

The Islam preaches the theory that it is the only true faith in this world. It shares this opinion with the Witnesses of Jehovah, the fundamentalist Dutch Protestant churches, The Mormons and Catholics where it concerns themselves. But when other religions show a certain tolerance towards other religions, Muslims do not need to. They are not obligated to loyalty to heathen. This means that agreements with heathen can be renounced if there is no more need. And the Muslim remains perfectly honest in Muslim eyes. This is the reason that a Muslim immigrant in Europe can marry a European girl, have children with her and after a while takes his children to his country of origin and forget all about his marriage. The country of origin, usually Morocco, Algeria, Egypt or Turkey, does not cooperate with the European country to have the children returned to the European country. Or that a Moroccan, who works in a European country, claims to have 15 children in Morocco for which he requests the usual children allowance. The authorities in Morocco feel, as Muslims, perfectly honest when they provide the paperwork to prove that the requester has indeed 15 children. Even if the man is only 32 years old and has no children at all. They may feel honest because there is for them no obligation of honesty towards heathen and if heathen provide a man with thousands of florins or francs on a simple piece of paper, they may.

If I would write this to a newspaper and had it printed, I would be prosecuted immediately for discrimination because every Muslim organization would appeal to the European laws concerned. Of course if you would tell the world that the USA is involved in a war against the Islam, the building of the UN would explode for the same reason.

The Islam world in common considers the western world as an easy money provider. Development Aid comes from the western world, although many countries that enjoy this aid are Muslim countries. The world sees the International Red Cross to provide emergency aid all over the world, but you ever saw a plane of the Red Crescent on a western world disaster spot bringing goods? Even if in Lebanon some disgusting religious event takes place on which mothers cut the heads of their baby sons to bleeding and show them proudly to reporters of European newspapers, it is the Red Cross who provides medical aid. Not the Red Crescent.

The general idea is, that the western world, and then especially the former colonial countries before the Second world war and the US after, is responsible for all disaster in the world and they should pay for it.

In countries where Muslims are a minority, they usually are willing and cooperative with the heathen majority. This lasts only to the moment they become majority themselves. Then the slightest offense sets off a Muslin fury with usually the

Christians and other heathen as victims of such a kind that Himmler, had he be alive, would beg on his knees to ask the Muslims how they got such marvelous ideas. Examples for that are Sudan, Nigeria, Indonesia, Malaysia, the Philippines, and, at present, Macedonia and Kosovo.

Muslims, as a minority, like to act as innocent underdogs and mosques are found all over the world. But no Christian church is found in Arabia.

The days after the 11th of September, all Muslims in Europe pulled their heads between their shoulders and took a low profile. Except in those cities with large quarters of Muslims. There they cried out their joy openly. In many Muslim countries the same was seen. After some days and because you did not react immediately, all the Muslim world, including Muslims in European countries, begun to express their regrets about the events, at the same time telling that is was America's guilt. By now (16 October) they show quit an aggressive attitude towards people who put the quilt on the eternal hate campaign as is taught on Muslim schools in Muslim countries **and** in Europe. The fear for reactions is gone and that's it.

THE ISLAM IN EUROPE

At the end of the years '60 a new phenomenon occurred in Europe. Low tech laborers became scarce because socialist laws made it easy to stop working. Instead of that, someone could easily get an allowance that made good enough living. Examples:

- A BOM-woman (BOM= Bewust Ongehuwd Moeder = Wittingly Unmarried Mother) became pregnant and claimed not to be able to work anymore because she had to take care of the baby. The result was a minimum allowance and children allowance which together made an easy life.

- A painter for indoor work came without employment and got automatically an unemployment allowance. When employment was offered in an outdoor job, the man refused that, claiming that he was an indoor painter.
- A person in his fifties became unemployed. Because there was little to no change that he ever could find employment again, he was partially declared disabled. (Usually problems of the back, the lungs, blood circulation etc.) The result was an allowance for not being able to work on medical criteria. The difference in total between unemployment allowance and allowance for being disabled was remarkable.

In fact in almost all of the present countries of the European Union existed a vast population of allowance takers. You understand that employers became desperate. It is clear that many of these allowance takers made an extraordinary good living by doing some black labor. The BOM-mother received regularly a 'friend', the painter painted for half price etc.

Employers started to seek employees in Mediterranean countries. Those were usually Morocco and Turkey. After a not too long time, the so-called guest laborers, mainly Muslims, became part of the different communities. They kept up a low profile, spoke hardly the language of the country where they lived and tried not to draw attention.

The intention was to let them work for a couple of years and then have them repatriated. But while working in Europe they paid social taxes and thus acquired certain rights. After some time it became clear that they could not be repatriated without violating their rights. They asked for reunion of the family, which was on humanity grounds allowed, and a stream of spouses came to the different European countries. These spouses did not speak the language of their new land and on religious grounds were not allowed to take part in any education program. The need to integrate in the European society disappeared with the arrival of the women. Muslim quarters became large communities. In fact the different Muslim nationalities simply created a piece of their own land within the borders of another.

Because they also had to pay the so called Church taxes, they asked and got their Mosques. Once they got them, they used a lack of Muslim education in the schools to ask for Muslim teachers. They got them. But a Muslim in a Catholic or Protestant school causes problems. Especially when female teachers are involved. Some disgusting things happened at the different schools, many schools refused Muslim children with the excuse that they had already too many and the Muslims asked for special Muslim schools. They got them. 2/3 of these schools in Belgium don't want any subsidy from the government. That enables them to refuse school inspections from that government.

I dare to say that these schools are a source of anti American propaganda. The products of this schools are usually to be found at night at the streets, harassing other people, causing problems in bars and nightclubs (What does a Muslim with a beer in one hand and an imitation hamburger, made of pork, in the other?) so that they are refused entree the next time and because of the refusal causing riots. This contingent of Muslims and their breed is in the years '80 and '90 reinforced by asylum seekers of, also, mainly Muslim countries. They claim to be prosecuted for their religion or for political affairs. One might think that a refuge who escapes Iran, Iraq, Afghanistan or one of the other countries, is already glad when gets into a neighbor land. But they arrive in Europe in planes. Some remarkable examples:

- In Holland we had Afghani, who escaped Afghanistan during the Russian war **and** their torturers, who flew for the Taliban, in one camp. So Holland had the war criminal in his hand and did not prosecute or refuse him or send him back. Both got finally the so called Status A, which means that they got the minimum allowance for living and were allowed to find a house, employment etc.
- Holland had more than 10 cases in which African (mainly Muslims) Asylum seekers asked, during their stay in a camp and awaiting Status A, for transsexual operations. Because the law does not allow discrimination and they were entitled to medical aid, they got it. After their operations they were refused asylum and went back to their countries without fear. The very expensive operation was all they wanted.
- Regularly it was found out that asylum seekers, after receiving Status A, went on vacation to the country that supposed to prosecute them.

By now, the Muslim population in Europe is that vast, that illegal immigrants find easily jobs and housing in the Muslim community wherever they want. Very often they don't need or want contact with the original population. They exist in vast Muslim communities where even the police does not like to inspect.

In Belgium, and I calculated this with help of articles in news papers during some months, roughly 60 percent of all crimes is committed by people of Muslim origin while being only 8 percent of the population. Legal and illegal. Quit a lot of Muslims became members of political parties. Those are usually the socialist and former communist (Greenies) parties. At the beginning of the years '90 is was fashion in European politics that every party had his own Turk or Moroccan. It was a prove of tolerance, cooperation with a minority and a broad mind. Of course it was a nice way to enlarge the electorate. In The Netherlands some Turkish gangsters infiltrated that way in the socialist party in the nineties.

The elected Muslim politician usually keeps himself busy with defending his own electorate and desperately looking for one of the well paying political jobs in the enormous amount of committees, advisory organizations and other money making affairs. Especially the Belgian politicians make him or her good example. Many of the socialist party and the Christen democrat party were prosecuted for corruption. I personally think that, had the Russians offered more money, the Belgian Air Force would fly by now Hinds and Migs instead of Augusta's and Mirages. And in their Belgian way they would have motivated that afterwards. But for the Muslim politician it are good examples and for sure reason to place himself on a pedestal of honesty because he can never hope to be involved in such a corruption deal.

But in general may be said that Muslim politicians are accepted, work well and have a lot of influence on their community.

Unfortunately, they have also a lot of rational influence on their socialist colleagues. It surprised me that, some days after the events, many greenies and socialist politicians throughout Europe repeated in fact the Muslim expressed reasons why the US is to be blamed itself for the terrorist attacks. Obviously all left wing parties tend to howl with the strongest anti American voice.

What surprised me also is, that the young Muslim people, born and raised in a Western country and having adopted a western way of life, so totally have chosen the side of a, to them, totally unknown people and with the wrong arguments. Quote: 'The Americans have to blame themselves because they are responsible for the struggle between Palestinians and Jews, are responsible for the massacres in Rwanda and the poverty in the third world. And I don't believe that Bin Laden had done this. I believe it is an Israeli conspiracy.' Unquote.

Another remarkable observation is, that in many simple Muslim eyes The US is not so much a country as well as an evil phenomenon. They do not talk about Americans as the subjects of a country but as a group of people with always bad intentions. Already in the nineties, when I had discussions with Dutch Muslim soldiers and pointing out the fact that, had the US not taken part in the war against the Third Reich, there would not have been a Muslim minority in Europe because they would have followed the Jews via the chimney of an incinerator, they argued that in all wars the US had only their own advantage in mind. In fact, arguing with a Muslim about Americans is the same as trying to get a Witness of Jehovah with his two legs on the ground again.

The whole of the reaction of Muslim Europe on the events of the 11th of September gives the impression of being orchestrated. It is probably not, but the Muslim scholars have done their job.

One other remarkable point is, that Muslim women are not available to non-Muslim men. A Turkish father rather kills his daughter than allowing her a marriage with a Christian. This has happened several times throughout European countries. It causes a self-explanatory friction between young Muslims and Christian. Without trying to be cynical, I may say that in general young Muslims use non-Muslims girls as a kind of sperm collection bags and afterwards dropping them with the garbage.

Since the years '70 becoming a Muslim seems to be a phenomenon of fashion, a misplaced show of philosophy or as a protest against western values. This in Europe as well as in the US. This kind of people is not taken very serious in the Muslim world. A blond Dutchman with his Dutch habits who becomes Muslim and wants to marry a Muslim girl is still hardly acceptable for her parents.

As I mentioned, Muslims have no loyalty left for heathen

THE EUROPEAN COUNTRIES

The first thing, Mr. President, you must have noted is that the Prime Minister of Belgium in his different statements **never** stated that **Belgium** as a sovereign country is standing right behind the US. He states that the European Union is standing behind the US. When he says 'we', he talks as chairman of the EU. He never stated that the European Union is standing absolutely and without restrictions behind the US. As chairman of the EU he made immediately a statement that this 'standing behind' concerns the fight against terrorism.

And after some days he enfeebled that 'standing behind' by stating that terrorist who will be arrested in Europe, will not be delivered to the US because they might get a dead penalty. This automatically means that your investigating services cannot give any information to their European colleagues because you must fear that the terrorist will be arrested in Europe.

Except for the British, Europe has proven his solidarity with the US mainly verbal.

The EU has his decision making process in common with that of NATO and the UN. This organizations have always splendid excuses to do nothing if it is not their advantage by declaring that 'it has to be negotiated", "it has to be thought over", "it must be unanimously get approval from all members of the organization", "This is not the organization to decide about that", etc.

Having a closer look at the individual countries, their opinions concerning the events of the 11th of September and their behavior in the past, I am afraid that we have now kicked open one of that doors of which we do not like to look behind.

Belgium

This country is known for its famous political decision making process. After the US forces, with the loss of thousands of soldiers, liberated this land, everybody was eternally grateful. Women showed their gratitude towards their liberators by offering themselves and thus helping to create a baby boom and their husbands closed their eyes for it because they wanted to share in the famous chocolate, food, cigarette, nylon stocking and alcohol flow. Not unrealistic in that circumstances of course. Personally I think that the funds for the Star Wars Program would be hardly sufficient if the US had to pay for the pensions of all this 'unknown' American Belgians who are, this must be said, my age. I want to emphasize here and now that I am a perfect look alike of my father.

After the end of that war Belgium became one of the most pro American countries in Europe. Except of course the citizen who had been collaborators with the Germans, the communists and the pro French Walloons.

With the beginning of the European Community for Carbon and Steel, their interest in America begun to fade away. Europe was closer and offered more opportunity for Belgium to win influence with its economical advantages. Belgium started to collect international institutions on its soil. When President De Gaulle threw the NATO, SHAPE and AFCENT out of France because he was not allowed involvement in the US/UK nuclear program, Belgium was quite willing to accept that organizations in Brussels and Mons. For Belgium, all this international organizations prove that the country is indeed the 'heart' of Europe. Besides that, the vast staffs of these organizations make exceptional remuneration's and give a lot of employment. The fact that such organizations are also a cause of wasted funds, corruption, theft and favoritism, fitted perfectly the Belgian mentality. The Belgian Prime Minister VandenBoeynants of the years '60 was, in the '90, sentenced 3 years conditional for tax evasion. But he is never sentenced for expropriating the houses of thousands of Belgians in Brussels, buying their houses and ground cheap via a real estate organization and selling the ground exceptional expensive to the city of Brussels to build the buildings for this international organizations. Belgian history since then shows a row of this kind of political misbehavior which ended with the famous Agusta and Dassault affaires, which took the political heads of several socialist politicians, ending with Willy Claes being by that time the Secretary-general of NATO. The opinion that this behavior only concerns politicians is wrong. The mentality is rooted in almost every soul in Belgium. When PM Martens in December 1990 refused the deliverance of 155mm Howitzer ammunition to the UK, is was because the Belgian government was involved in negotiations with the Palestinians to free the Belgian Jewish Houtekins family, who was taken hostage by the Palestinians and had an envoy send to Saddam Hussein to let Belgian hostages in Iraq go. Shortly after the refusal to deliver ammunition to the UK, the family was free. When NATO requested Belgium, during the same period, a contribution to the ACE MOBILE FORCE in favor of Turkey, Martens hesitated and claimed that the Diyarbakir Airfield had to be inspected to see if it could support the Belgian F-16 squadron. I seem to remember that this decision took him 11 days. He could have had the answer via a simple phone call from me in the five minutes I needed to find the last inspection report. And he must have known that. If you think that this was an honest man who only tried to serve his country in what he thought was the best way, please Mr. President, forget that. He was a creep who had, as a married christen politician, a sexual affair with his second in the CVP party during 10 years, after which period he started another love affair with some younger woman and finally divorced his wife and married that last young flower. If you think this is a matter of gossip, ask your intelligence services. And I do not mention this to shock. Since Mr. Clinton you cannot be shocked anymore. I want you to be aware of the kind of people you are dealing with.

Between the 20th and the 24th of December 1990 US, UK, NL and German officers openly declared that NATO and SHAPE should leave Belgium immediately and be transferred to another and loyal country.

The Gulf war was, in Belgium, generally considered to be a war to keep the deliverance of oil to the US guaranteed. The government never tried to change that opinion of the population by some official explanation. Of course they were loyal and offered contribution. A minesweeper and plaster. Of course they will offer, in your fight against terrorism, a contribution. I hope there is some lake in Afghanistan for their minesweeper.

In general, the Belgian government has only two goals: Making their country the political center of Europe and their economical advantages. And this prior to loyalty or the defense of western values.

Belgium remains Belgium as long as the Flemish part of the country allows the flow of billions of francs to the French speaking Walloons. In 2000, during a session of the parliament, the Walloon PM threatened the Flemish to split the country and join France if the solidarity between the Dutch speaking part and the French speaking part of the country ceased to exist. The answer of a Flemish politician was remarkable. Quote: "Please do so and take that King with you." Unquote.

Belgium has 7 full organized parliaments and six governments, besides the county governments of course. They do not exist to manage the country in a better way, but only to create well paid jobs for thousands of low quality politicians.

Officially, there were no signs of solidarity with Bin Laden within the Muslim community. But the Muslims I spoke to (an Algerian waiter in a restaurant in Givet where my wife and I regularly use a dinner, a Pakistani Gasoline station owner in Loverval where I regularly replenish my car and a Moroccan who was reading a newspaper with the facts of the 11th in a road restaurant and thus offering me the possibility to ask him what he thought about it, had all the same explanation. It was America's own guilt etc. Had I have the opportunity to talk to more Muslims, I would have had for sure the same answers.

Germany

After World War 2, Germany felt guilty of crime without precedence. That was a general idea and forced upon them by the conquerors. Of course there was some logic in it. Together with Japan the Germans were responsible for 52 million people killed during the war. But there was also a sentiment that injustice was done to very young men who, under the standards of the SS had given their lousy 17 and 18 years for their homeland. As a former German artillery officer in 1962 told me: Quote: "I only had a few cannons left. But to keep them only for 20 minutes longer in firing position to allow some units a safe withdraw, I saw a full company of the Waffen SS running into Russian fire to keep them off. No one survived." Unquote.

Heroism or fanaticism for a wrong ideal, the Germans paid their price.

After the war, many Germans accepted the occupation of their land as a natural result of their misbehavior and adapted to the kind of freedom as the US occupation forces displayed The result was the Wirtschaftswunder or, as a free translation, the business miracle. Willingly they accepted the quilt of their past and cooperated in every sense to make Europe a safer place to live. Maybe it was French initiative to unite Europe, but it was German money that made it possible. The Germans paid for the unity of Europe, for the Jewish victims, for the damage in the European countries and in fact they were sucked out by those countries. They were for a long time the most loyal NATO members. Until Chancellor Helmut Kohl saw in 1990 a possibility to reunite East and West Germany again. That afforded in fact more money than West Germany could afford, with the result that some financial contributions to the EU could not be made. Europe was angry. How dared that Boches (an abusive French word for Germans) refuse a request for money? Europe forgot that the Germans had, in their feelings of being guilty, already paid them poor. It was not a surprise that the Germans decided, after the nasty remarks of Europe, that they had already paid enough and started to have a closer look at their own interest. Their attitude towards Europe changed and although they are still loyal Europeans, they begun to consider themselves more important than the smaller countries, which is in fact true.

Without Germany and its economy, an EU cannot exist. This also thanks to the personal friendship between Kohl and Mitterrand. Especially the French President had an important influence on Kohl. He convinced Kohl that France and Germany, together with maybe Italy to make the affair look more legal, easily could run Europe without much participation of the smaller countries. The lucky event of the dead of Mitterrand and shortly after that the reassignment of Kohl, caused by his corruption, ended the affair.

Germany still shows certain honesty in its political decision making process towards Europe, NATO and the US and is, once committed, reliable.

France

It is not the French who liberated France. I never understood why Gen. Eisenhower allowed Gen. De Gaulle to enter Paris as first. If I wring a whale, I see the quantity of US-spoiled blood wasted for the liberation of France. To see the French spoiled blood for that country, I only need to wring a mouse.

The general idea in France, concerning their liberation is, that they did that with 'some American assistance'.

Besides that there are vast Muslim communities in France, it has some ideas in common. One of these ideas is that French culture is the most important, oldest and leading culture in the western world. You might speak French, Mr. President, you can speak with the French but you cannot communicate with them. Everybody in this world has two nationalities, his own and the French. As long as you confirm their cultural superiority.

The 'Alliance Française' is an organization all over the world that promotes the French language. If you would follow those lessons, you will find out that in that lessons, obviously only meant to teach someone a foreign language, is a superb program of indoctrination in French culture. To spread that culture they force all organizations in the world to accept French as an official language. Muslims have the same idea about their religion.

If you call the UN in New York, the first question you hear is whether you want to talk English or French. Every document in the EU must be translated in French and during my 7 years at SHAPE I have thrown away enough French documents (because the Staff officers preferred waiting for the English translation) without reading, to have sufficient fuel to steam the Kitty Hawk from New York to Afghanistan and back.

One third of the working budget of the EU is paid for translation. (The rest is mainly used to pay for TDY's that are never made by the travelers and foolish high working funds. One of the US agents could easily find out that every parliamentary representative gets the equivalent of about HFL 20.000,00 per month to run his office. He will also discover that many European parliamentarians use their mother officially as a typist, their 16 year old brother or sister as clerk and their poor 96 year old grandfather, who has artificial dents, walks with walking sticks and is incontinent, as assistant.

For the parliamentarians of the South-European countries it means 'normal businesses. For the French, who stand a bit closer to the North-European mentality, it means only that they have to be more careful. They know that they are doing wrong but the flesh is weak and everybody is doing it. So What?

But had the French language be skipped as official language, the saved money in the UN, the EU and at NATO could remit the debts of one development country every year. And those organizations would not function worse. It is not the French that pay for this nonsense but the international community.

I know that the Americans have a weak spot for the French. Maybe because of the Liberty Statue, maybe because of Lafayette. Less known is that Lafayette was a French dagger in the back of the UK. When later on the US grew, Napoleon the Third had no problems with offering Maximilian of Austria the non existing emperor's crown of Mexico, knowing that it would cause problems for the US. Maximilian only had to conquer the country.

If one country in Europe gives priority to its own business, it is France. Indeed it cooperated in the Gulf war coalition. But only to show their importance and for sure to take care of their interests in the Middle East countries. They were quit sour when it turned out that Arabia bought only US military equipment after the war. I seem to remember that the rumors, that the US had gained more of the war than it has cost them, started in France.

When the Srebrenica affair happened, The Dutch troops were under French command. During those days a US Aircraft carrier was in the Mediterranean. I was by that time already dismissed from the Crisis Management Center of the Ministry of Defense but had the result already foreseen and expressed to my superiors in the Defense Crisis Management Center.

I told my superior that the Dutch commander should ask direct help from the US to safe his battalion and the habitants of the enclave. It would have been easy with US planes to protect a corridor from Srebrenica to the Bosnian border. It was about 30 kilometers and the US could have kept that corridor safe for 24 hours. The advice was obviously never relayed. It might be that, because the advice came from a person who committed high-treason, it was not acceptable. Maybe because a man with the rank of a Sergeant-major is not supposed to posses the right knowledge, but it would have saved 6000 men. It would also have put the qualities of the French commander in spotlights.

The simple Frenchman might have a weak point for the US, but the politicians do not.

As this document is not a lesson in terror, it is also not meant as a lesson in history. But questioning a historian concerning France-US relations, you will find out that this relation was always the advantage of France or it did not exist.

I was shocked when I saw you together with the French president during your visit to Europe. It might be that diplomatic customs forced you. But you should remember that a picture was published in the newspapers on which the president of the United States was displayed with a man who is only escaping trial for corruption because he legislated a law that does not allow a reigning president to be brought to trial. In the street he would be, and actually is called, a crook.

If the French see a possibility to weaken the influence of the US in the world or the leadership of the US in NATO, they use that possibility

The vast Muslim communities in the south of France openly expressed their joy about the events of the 11th of September. The French government did not react.

France should not considered being a loyal country. To none.

The Netherlands

The Netherlands is an uncomplicated country. Not because it is my homeland and thus easy to understand for me, but because its history is simple. The common Dutchman can be characterized as follows: A Dutchman buys from a Jew, sales to a Scott and still makes profit. It might be not the finest way to describe the Dutch as a people, but it describes exactly their mentality.

The basis for this country was laid in the 16th century when the Dutch, after 80 years of war, threw out the Spaniard and became independent. Although William of Orange, a German noble, was the driving mechanism behind that fight for freedom, it took more than 150 years before the Dutch accepted one of the descendants of that man to be King of the Netherlands. The country has been for a long time a republic and that republic was based on their Calvinist religion and the United East-Indian Company (VOC). When the Dutch Navy was a feared power in the world, it had not been established to enforce Dutch superiority. It was generally paid for by the VOC and only to protect communication lines. The Netherlands never conquered their colonies. Wars like the UK Army fought to conquer India and its neighbor countries were unacceptable to the VOC council. Simply because wars cost money. The purpose of the VOC was to make money, not war.

Because of that vision, to protect the communication lines, Holland became a world power only by coincidence.

Had Peter Stuyvesant found in New Amsterdam a source of wealth for the VOC, (for the America's was established the West Indian Company) New York would have still be called New Amsterdam and the US was not established after a revolution against the UK but after a revolution against the Netherlands.

Had Maurits The Brazilian, a bastard son of William of Orange, (are all men with a disgusting sexual behavior called Bill?) been a bit more scientific and less bellicose, he would have found in Brazil immense sources of wealth for the VOC and Brazil would have spoken Dutch by now and not Portuguese. The VOC usually gave up any piece of territory once it obviously turned out to be worthless to them.

The Netherlands is a Kingdom, but the Dutch are no monarchists. They are Orangists. They feel very strongly attracted by the House of Orange. When in the years '70 the socialist party with a party leader, whose name was Den Uyl, (The man who did not want US Neutron grenades and cruise missiles on Dutch soil) included in their program the abolishment of the Royal house, a poll showed a loss of about 60 percent of their electorate. He called the abolishment program a mistake and canceled it. Shortly after he took revenge by accusing Prince Bernhard of the Netherlands to be corrupted by Lockheed.

The Netherlands never took much care of their defense. With the philosophy that the UK could not allow France or Germany to conquer Holland, Germany could not allow the UK or France to do it, the Netherlands have always been quit defenseless but, living in peace, balancing on a needle of political tensions in Europe. This lasted till the Second World War. Hitler had other ideas about neutrality.

The Second World War which brought the loss of our Jewish community in Amsterdam in 1941, brought also many Dutch to resistance. Before the deportation of the Jews, there was hardly any resistance against the Germans. Afterwards maybe too much, because the resistance caused extreme harassment from the German side with the result that too many innocent Dutch useless paid with their lives. But Germany triggered that resistance because they violated the deepest feelings of the Dutch that includes the idea that everybody who enjoys Dutch hospitality, every refuge who looks in his needs for shelter and care, should be safe in the Netherlands. This has been so for hundreds of years. The Pilgrim Fathers sailed from Holland to New England, being prosecuted in England.

The Dutch always have been reasonable loyal NATO members. Even in the time when Cruise missiles should be stocked on our soil and many peace organizations resisted that idea. Remarkable is, that the common professional Dutch soldier considers himself a better soldier than those of the rest of NATO and for sure better than those of the US. The reason for that idea is that the different wars the US were involved in, caused many losses on US side. But the Dutch had no wars to fight after the Korea involvement. So we had no losses. We could say about this that, if you don't stick your nose in dangerous business, you don't get a fist on it.

Contrary to the French, The Netherlands considers NATO still to be the best guarantee for peace. They have that in common with the other smaller countries. Maybe because they don't want to rely on the French who, with no doubt, will try to take the leadership in a European Defense Organization. That's why, for instance, the West European Union never became an effective power.

In general could be said that The Netherlands are loyal to NATO but "please, don't expect too much from us because we are only a collection of poor grocery owners who only want to make a buck, drink a glass of jenever and smoke our Gouda pipes".

After 1990 and the fall of communism it was under Minister of Defense Relus Ter Beek, a socialist, that the defense organization of The Netherlands was totally excavated. In parliament he claimed that The Netherlands finally could take their 'Peace' dividend and promptly the other ministers fought for the bits and pieces of the Defense budget. After a year and doing nothing to stop the process, Ter Beek finally declared that if the budget was further lowered he would not take the responsibility. For him an old dream came true. He is no doubt a favorite of the 'broken rifle' group.

In The Netherlands are now more Generals than companies sergeant-majors of fighting units. His successor, Minister Voorhoeve, could have expected the equivalent of a Formula 1 racing car after all the promises of Ter Beek to modernize the Dutch forces.

He inherited a rusty bicycle.

I think there is no need to talk about other countries. The North European countries are more reliable. The South European countries can only be bought with dollars or economical advantages. You only should remember the Greek socialist Papandreou and his election promises to 'throw' the

Yankees out of Greece and close the USAF bases. After he was elected the disgusting negotiations started and the Bases remained open to, I believe a price of 600 million dollar. As usual with socialists in Europe, later on the man was accused of theft of government money, divorced his wife and took some prostitute as companion. The French Mitterrand was his great example.

THE UNITED NATIONS
Where NATO and the EU are organizations that offer a platform for a certain amount of corrupt politicians, The UNO is an organization that forces honest and well meaning politicians to accept the presence of political hoodlums.
In it's about 55 years of existence, it has attained almost nothing.
Does Israel live within safe borders?
Is Tibet freed from the Chinese?
Are those infernal goats in the Maghreb-countries exterminated?
Has discrimination ceased to exist?
Has the caste system in India ceased to exist?
Do we have all warlords isolated and powerless?
Is the abuse of children as cheap labor or sexual prey stopped?
Do not anymore 30.00 children per day die because of a simple lack of potable water?
Did we stop the Muslims to execute their disgusting genital mutilation of very young girls?
Have we condemned the many countries who forbid white citizen and habitants to posses' real estate?

Have we arrested and tried the so-called strong men during the past 40 years in Africa who initiated massacres and committed tribal murder?

Was Pol Pot hunted down?

Has the UN done in fact anything to make this world any better?

For sure not.

It is thanks to the UN that all this things happen.

The UN forbids the intervention without permission in other countries because it would be violation of sovereignty. But in the past only a few battalions of well trained forces were already capable of stopping the disastrous regimes of Idi Amin, of Kwame Nkuma, or, even by now, Mugabe. A coalition like that of the Gulf war could have stopped Pol Pot, could have united Korea, and could have ended Mobutu. But the UN did not and does not.

The grimy cultures of the nomads in the Maghreb countries with their goats are responsible for the enlargement of the Sahara Desert by about 20.000 square kilometers per year. The contamination of the Great Lakes of Africa by the dead bodies thrown in of, during tribal wars killed people, causes wretched sicknesses. The animal-like sexual behavior creates the biggest epidemic of AIDS in the world. Dictators all over the world care only for their bank accounts on European banks, causing innumerable casualties per year in their countries and still are in power.

Muslim terrorists like Arafat were and are treated like honorable guests in Europe and the US. (But I still see the US disabled veteran on the Achille Lauro who was thrown overboard during a hijack of that ship by PLO-terrorists. I still see the US marine colonel swaying and turning in his rope in Lebanon after being killed by Muslim terrorists.)

I can't even understand that Arafat ever was allowed to set foot on US territory without being arrested.

Dictatorial regimes send their ambassadors to the UN in New York and are accepted as speaking partners.

Totally inane persons as the Dutch Minister of Environment Pronk were in their younger years working for the UN in Geneva (under the disreputable M'Bow) to a salary of the equivalent of Hfl 500.000,00 a year besides fringe benefits during which period of ten years he acquired a liking for traveling on UN account. And that for the real socialist.

I have seen advertisements in Dutch newspapers that asked for money because: Quote 'for HFL 1,95 we can cure a child in the third world of leprosy'. Unquote.

A simple calculation teaches me that, had Pronk only accepted the also good wage of HFL 50.000,00 a year and giving the rest available to the purpose of curing children in the 3th world of leprosy, in his ten years he would have made it possible to cure more than 2.225.000 children of leper. Had M'Bow done the same, the problem had been solved all over the world.

This same minister blames the US for all the evil in the world, including the global pollution, on the Kyoto conference. Obviously, in his ten years at Geneva he has done nothing because all the problems, he had to take care of, are not solved.

Had the UN not existed, there would have been less problems in this world because every country would have been extremely careful not to offense or menace another country. In these modern times with its weapons for retaliation, bilateral treaties would have worked much better than resolutions of the UNO. Has the US not been present in Europe, the USSR would not have been stopped to conquer Europe by a UNO resolution. It were not the Hammarskjold's, the Oe Thant's, Kiesingers, Ghalis and Annans who kept Europe free from occupation by the USSR. It were the Eisenhowers, Kennedy's, Johnson's, Nixons, and Reagans who did. The Gulf war did, in fact, not need the approval of the UN. Dictators would not as easily as these days had been capable of having bank accounts in democratic countries because local laws these days forbid the transfer, white wash and possession of, what is in fact, black money. It is not the UN but a change in moral standards that have initiated those laws. Bilateral agreements and treaties between democratic countries would have been much better guarantees for safety than the UN ever can give. The expensive UN organization would not have swallowed the money that better had been used for those who really needed it. Countries would have had more control on how their money for development aid was spend. That excessive wages of the personnel of the organization, their buildings, their cars, their secretaries with or without cigars, would not have been taken from the poorest in this world.

There is hardly a country to find in this world that executes the resolutions of the UN, because they don't fear this powerless organization. They only fear for one member: The

US. And if the US does not react, nothing happens. And if the US reacts, they usually are criticized for doing it not good.

Mr. President, you might think of the following examples:

- After the founding and recognition by the UNO of the state of Israel, the Jews established a democratic state in every sense of the word. The Arabs never stopped their terrorist activities towards this democratic country. The UNO never reacted properly. The US did and became since then permanent under Muslim verbal fire. Not exactly democratic regimes themselves.
- Besides terrorist attacks Israel had to fight several wars to rescue its existence. The UNO never reacted properly.
- Terrorists may move freely within Muslim countries and plan their activities without being arrested. (During the Gulf war a Dutch Newspaper displayed the house and way of living of the female terrorist 'Leila' in Damascus. She lives there as a normal citizen, brings her children to school and behaves as if she has nothing to fear. She **has** nothing to fear.) The UN does not react. One might expect that, when a reporter can find this out, the UNO can. (and the CIA for sure).
- The UNO condemns the use of children for war purposes. The PLO under Arafat does. The UNO does not react. During the war between Iraq and Iran, the latter used the children by thousands. The UNO did not react.
- It is forbidden to discriminate because of religion, gender, color of skin, origin or political opinion. China discriminates on political grounds, the Muslim countries for religious reasons, many countries on color of skin, all Muslim countries on gender. The UNO never reacts.
- The treaty of New York of 1957 never mentioned homosexuality as a gender. But since then homosexuals consider themselves to be a separate gender. In Europe

the most disgusting things happened and happen around homosexuals. And I am sure that the same happens in the US and all over the world. No one ever reacts. We have separated facilities for men and women. But how would you feel if, after coming back from military exercise and taking a shower with your squad, platoon or whatever the unit is, and you feel the eyes of a homosexual going over your body? But a report to the commanding officer only results in a silence. A fat Minister of Defense considers it to be normal. The UNO never corrected that homosexual point of view.

In the UNO every vote has the same value. Nice for the US, Mr. President. It means that your voice has the same value as that of Jerry Rawlins, Mugabe, and the rulers, whoever they may be, of Mali, Nepal and the different Shitstans, the Prince of Liechtenstein and the rulers of former Dutch Surinam. All countries have the same rights. There must fall a stone from your hearth because, now I have told you, the US can withdraw from its responsibilities and starting to take care of itself. All that important countries may take over the burden of paying for all kind of peacekeeping organizations, sending forces to all kind of problem spots on the globe, settle the Middle East problems and in general take care of the well functioning of the UN.

I will use a word to describe my opinion about that equality of UN members of which I think is a very proper American expression because I heard it very often be used by high-ranking US superiors at SHAPE in discussions with European Officers.

Bullshit.

It may be said that the UNO never attains his goals, causes much more problems in the world than had been there without the UNO and supports regimes that fulfill all characteristics to have them prosecuted as once the Third Reich rulers have been.

UNITED STATES AS A NOTION

After the Isolation between the world wars and the involvement of the US with the world since World War 2, for many simple people in the world the US became something else as a country. It started with the idea that the US was a kind of Salvator Mundi. It saved half of Europe of the ideas of Hitler, saved that saved half of the ideas of Stalin and his successors, brought that saved half again on its economical legs with the Marshall plan and brought totally new ideas to Europe. The 'American way of life' was for a longer time an adored item in Europe. The result was a bulk of emigrants from Europe to the US in the fifties. The US enforced the European countries to give their colonies sovereignty in an outburst of idealism and slowly the world settled down in East and west and North and south. The strong men in Africa came to power and half of them were the result of indoctrination by the USSR. The NATO, CENTO and SEATO kept the USSR from the oceans and many rulers changed their minds and fell for wealth and power from the USSR instead of that from the US and in a reasonable short time the US had to use all its diplomatic power to control that process.

Had the Korean War been an acceptable UNO war to the world, the Vietnam War was not an acceptable SEATO war. Everywhere in Europe anti-war, anti US-organizations came to flower (In the Netherlands the well known Pronk, his party member Relus Ter Beek and other socialists were the first in line during anti-US demonstrations. During the change of presidency in the US (Johnson>Nixon) I was, as a military policeman (Marechaussee) standing in front of the US Embassy in The Hague. And I was absolutely alone. I saw the demonstrators coming and taking position in front of the Embassy. I saw them having the usual rotten tomatoes and other fruits, stones and crowbars to break-up the streets and, reporting it, asked at the same time for a weapon and reinforcements. I was assured that I had nothing to fear and got the notice that I was not allowed to use my pistol. (I had only five rounds for thousands of demonstrators.) It was the US mariner who pulled me to safety a few seconds before almost every window was smashed by the waves of stones. In fact nothing happened to these demonstrators, although they had text plates with the remark: 'Johnson Murderer. Who's next.' and caused damage that was far beyond necessity to demonstrate.

Some weeks later I saw an article in a newspaper saying that a man had been condemned for offending a friendly statesman because, at the moment of the demonstrations in front of the US Embassy, that man had totally on his own demonstrated in front of the USSR Embassy with a text plate with the remark: 'Brezhnev murderer'.

All newspapers in Europe showed terrible pictures of casualties, caused by US bombing. I never saw the picture of a tortured body as victim of the NVA or the VC. The whole spirit of Europe seemed to be anti-US.

It was from hat time that the US changed from a friend, a liberator of Europe, a Salvator Mundi, to a notion. An American was not longer related to a country but to a phenomenon, an evil spirit that tried to rule the world that tried to force its opinion upon the world. It was one man and his armed forces.

It would have been easy for all European governments to start an enlightenment campaign via TV and radio to explain what the US was trying to do in Vietnam. What right it had to do what it did. That it had liberated Europe by the same means and that the governments were standing straight behind the US. They did not. Contrary to that, their silence was an approval for the behavior of those demonstrators.

It was clear that, when the Neutron grenade, the cruise missiles and Pershing missiles programs were started, the governments would have problems to explain why these weapons were needed. But it was coming from that awful entity that was called America so it was bad.

The by then Prime Minister Den Uyl called the neutron grenade a typical capitalist weapon. It killed people and saved material. He never explained that the weapon was needed to kill Red Forces on West-European soil without destroying our own cities after an eventual attack of the Warsaw-Pact on Western Europe.

As no other you will know that the toughs and opinions of politicians very often differ largely from that of the man in the street. In many countries in the world illiteracy is a widespread phenomenon and the opinions of the illiterates are mainly formed in Mosques, Temples, by left- and ultra right wing party demagogues and large pictures in newspapers. The communists with their Pravda, Mr. Goebbels with his Völkischer Beobachter and not to forget to mention the editors of the present newspapers in Europe who refer to you as a man who has 'excellent text writers', has excellent advisors, reads his text from an autocue, needs the hand of his father, confirmed dead penalties in the Lone Star State, knows nothing of foreign politics etc. are good examples of how public opinion can be influenced. Also by now you might notice that European governments never try to give a better vision on the US and his president to the public. Everybody seems to forget that you were Governor of a state of which the territory almost equals Germany and France together, has more habitants than most of the smaller European countries and that Lone Star State was better governed than that European countries. Every State in the US has one government. In Europe often and simply to create jobs for party members, you find governments of the type of an upside-down pyramid. And if no job can be found for the poor politician, it is created by establishing a committee for the welfare of frogs, tailless rats, short-sighted aged people of more than 100 years and hairless prostitutes. I wonder what would happen if I wrote an article in one of the most important newspapers of the US, telling that Spitaels, Claes, Chirac, Papandeou, and Craxi are and were corrupted crooks, Prince Philip of Belgium smiles after a joke one days after he heard it, the crown prince of Norway has married a woman with a bastard son and who was known for her obscene lifestyle and use of drugs. (I could mention a hundred or more cases) I think Europe would explode. But all that things are true and every intelligence agent on your European Embassies who reads newspapers can confirm that. But referring to the US President as a man with the intelligence of a toddler is fully acceptable in Europe and no one is ever prosecuted for offending that befriended statesman.

If I ask an acquaintance what the difference is between the bombing of Berlin, Hamburg, Leipzig, Dresden and further every industrial complex in Germany during World war 2 and the bombings on Northern Vietnam, Iraq and by now Afghanistan, I hear always the same answer. The first were absolutely necessary to stop a terrible regime and liberate Europe and the latter are and were not necessary because they served only the interest of the US. The German victims of the US bombings had to blame themselves because they started a war and Vietnam, Iraq and Afghanistan did not start a war. Vietnam was occupied by the US, there was no need to start the Gulf war because the US would have had his oil anyway and there was never a proof that the Taliban was involved in the events of the 11th of September. From the point of view of my speaking partners the US might have killed the whole population of Germany, included babies and children. But if one US bullet these days is fired in the wrong direction and hits a chicken, it is called an innocent life. The almost 5000 casualties of the Twin Towers do not matter. That was the US itself to blame. The conformity of the answers already gives an idea of the widespread of anti US indoctrination. And that answers come from Muslims and non Muslims alike. Mr. Goebbels would have admired it.

The European business man who regularly visits the US for his business does not share the points of view of those I talked to. That's right. And exactly he, and all those who have more or less intensive contacts with the US and its citizen do not share that views. But they are usually not the type of individuals who are easy indoctrinated. When I hear someone beginning with: "Yes, the terrorist attacks are terrible, but . . . . . .", then I know with what kind of people I am talking.

Indoctrination or simply howling with the wolves, it does not really matter because the result is the same: A strong and widespread anti American feeling that is not referred to a geographical spot on the globe but to a few men and women with an extremely strong military potential available to them.

I called it a notion.

THE UNITED STATES AND ITS PRESIDENT

When I state that the elections for a new President of the US attract as much attention in the world as it does in the US, I am not beside the true. Candidates for the job are analyzed in every newspaper in the world and the, for Europe and the rest of the world, undesired candidate is openly made as ridiculous as is possible. His past is dug up, his education is taken into account, his political views are messed-up and out of his history as politician the worst decisions are discussed. The US President is indeed as important to the world as it is to the US.

When the last elections were going on, I discussed it with a friend in the US and I stated that it would not matter for the US who would win. It would matter for the world.

A 'true' American, as the winner, irrespective who he is, is expected to be, will in the first place care for the US and its interests, then he will take care of the interests of the US again, then again, then five times nothing and finally the rest of the world will take his attention. And why should it be otherwise? If things go right in the US, it is also an advantage to the world. If things go wrong, it goes wrong in the rest of the world. But if the rest of the world is messing-up in the economical, political, military, religious and criminal sense, that same world blames the US President in particularly, the US in general or 'America' (as that notion) immediately and demands military intervention, economical help or political approval. And if a part of that world does not get what it wants, offenses, reproaches (Up to in the UNO) come out of the first drawer of every desk.

We might remember the Vietnam war, the oil-crisis in 1972, the Panama of Noriega, Granada, the Gulf war, Somalia and Yugoslavia. Even now the US is blamed for the bombing of Afghanistan. The Twin-towers are forgotten, the dead bodies become a statistic and Bin Laden is only a suspect to the world. The world is more occupied with what will happen to the poor victims of US bombings than with the lifetime mourning of those who lost his or her relatives in the towers. And in fact the world expects from the US that they pay for the damage in Afghanistan. Can you imagine a world in 1940 that tells Europe that it should pay for the costs of the war against them? Can you imagine Adenauer who tells the US that it should pay for the damages, caused by the bombings on Berlin, Hamburg, Dresden and Leipzig?

Fact is that the authority of the US President is, for the world, always in doubt. Had you done absolutely nothing in the sense of looking for moral support in the rest of the world but only address your citizen with the simple announcement that you will act in the proper way, the world would have been silent and tremble. When then missiles had been fired from US territory, disregarding the eventual casualties in Afghanistan, you would not have had worse reactions than you have know.

The fact that you sought moral support has weakened your position, allowed the world to tell you what to do and to criticize all your decisions after.

The US has suffered an immense financial loss. Why should the US pay for it? Why not tell the Muslim world that their interpretation of that religion caused your losses. Why should they not be forced to pay for the damage? Because you have made, with your decision to look for moral support, the US dependent on the worlds mercy. Every CIA report might have told you by now how much mercy the US may expect. Already by now I can predict that if ever Bin Laden will be available for trial, the world, and then especially the Muslim world because of their religion and Europe because they love fishing in troubled water, will look to it that Bin Laden is tried while regarding all his 'rights'. A good example of what will happen is the Lockerbie trial in Holland. Will that satisfy the survivors of the terrorist attacks? Will it prevent more attacks? Will it pay for that immense damage?

But a show is all the US will get.

Decisions of the President of the US almost always touch somehow the rest of the world. The following is at least worthwhile to consider:

1: I believe the time has come that the US President becomes untouchable.

2: I believe the time has come that the US will not rely anymore on the goodwill of the rest of the world

3: I believe the time has come that the US should quit with NATO and withdraw its military presence in Europe

4: I believe the time has come that the US end the presence of the UNO in New York and quit that miserable and money wasting organization.

5: I believe the time has come that the US pick up the attitude of that kind of men that made the US stretching from one ocean to another. Honest, reliable and their fears hidden behind their pressed-together teeth. That the US becomes independent again from the world and go back to their roots

Is that possible?

Will the world run smoothly without a UNO (because this organization will fall to pieces without the US), without a NATO (because it will become a powerless debating club without the US), without all kinds of agreements like the GATT, the environment conferences like that in Kyoto?

Will the US lose its economical, political and military influence in the world? I believe not.

I believe the world will really tremble if the US decides to withdraw from all that organizations.

Having a look at these options.

1: The President as untouchable. Some examples:

■ In a country, irrespective which one, the President of the US is offended. Every nasty remark might serve the purpose. The US withdraws their Embassy and the Ambassador of the concerned country becomes Persona

Non Grate. It might be that the government of that country remarks that the press in their country is free. But if the diplomatic relationship is not restored before the offender(s) is/are condemned, I am quite sure that the latter will take place to the satisfaction of the US rather quickly.

■ The President of the US is criticized for a decision by a foreign government. The head of state of that country is invited to the US to excuse the behavior of his government. He does not accept the invitation and that ends the diplomatic relation. It ends also the economical relation and all citizen of the concerned country are expelled from the US. The funds of that country in the US are frozen. I'll bet one month of my pension (I know, it is not much) to $1,00, that this head of state will accept that invitation before your secretary could calculate what the profit of our bet would be for you if that head of state would not show up.

A US President bears only responsibility for citizen of the US. They voted for him and they rely on him. Offending or criticizing the President of the US by a foreigner should be unacceptable to every American, Republican and Democrat alike. It is **their** president. Only **they** may criticize him and finally disapprove his decisions by not giving him a second term of office.

But the most important change would be that a law exists that:

The President of the United States will never be brought in a position in which he has to meet with, attends conferences on which is present, or is photographed together with: Any person who is known to have spilled blood of US citizen or

was involved in the event, is known for anti US expressions, is subject to criminal investigations, has been convicted for crimes or corruption or is known for his or her low moral standards

In practical terms today it means that you never have to meet Chirac again, never will meet the King of Belgium, and never will meet any Hezbolla, Jihad and Palestinian leader. I know. It will be a very messy job for the Vice President. But at least the world knows that the President of the US cannot be approached by any political crook.

Such a law will even have a remarkable influence on the world, because the citizen of countries of which the head of state or a self-declared VIP is not allowed access to the US President might wonder why the access is denied.

Will the US be called arrogant? Many newspapers have called America (that notion) to be arrogant since the Afghanistan war.

2: Goodwill

■ It were the European member-countries of NATO that relied on the US. Not in reverse. It is Israel that relies on the US. Not in reverse. And that counts for all countries that have a treaty for military support in case they are attacked. But where is the support for the US. During 50 years of NATO's existence, the US has paid 80% of its own presence in Europe. But it was Europe's safety to have the more than 300.000 US soldiers in Europe. Had there not been any US presence, the European countries would have had **all** the costs to maintain a much bigger army of their own When a US senator in 1992 asked the European countries to take a higher percentage in the costs of US presence, the request was denied. When Saudi Arabia was asked to give its territory available for the US forces after the terrorist attacks, it was denied because Afghanistan was a "Muslim country". Was in 1991 Iraq not a Muslim country?

- The US had to buy the 'approval' of Russia and the silence of China for the Gulf war. In fact, in every case the US need to act as a military power, some country tries to get economical advantages, political influence or simply direct aid in goods. The US never gets something as an act of friendship.
- The actions in Panama, Granada and Columbia were necessary. For the world this actions were not important. But the world condemned them because it gave a chance to criticize the US. The Dutch government (Lubbers) said that it 'understood' the actions and that was the general opinion of the Allies. But none said straight ahead: "O.K. Good action." It would have cost them nothing to declare that they were right standing behind the US.

The idea that the US can rely on the goodwill of the world is wishful thinking. The US has to pay for every bit of goodwill. Even if any US activity is in the interest of some country, other countries want a part of the booty. In fact the US does not need any goodwill. It should be the individual countries that should look for goodwill from the US.

3: Quit NATO

It was the military power of the US and the efforts of its war economy that liberated Europe. The countries with their 'headquarters' in London and their heads of state to create the usual political chaos would have remained there till now, had the US not done what it has done. Hitler would have created his Empire of thousand years and there would have been a united Europe with one head of state as the present heads of state pretend to desire. But the US did what it had done, suffering tenth of thousands of casualties throughout Europe and, after the war, created a situation in which Europe could flower. The ridiculous Western European Union, pretending to be the new military teeth of those European countries turned out to be dentures and was laid foundling. NATO was established and the US took the lead for about forty years. The US provided the nuclear umbrella for the NATO-members, paid for that and paid also for its own presence in Europe.

The first question that arises is: Were the European countries also loyal partners. Looking into history we must say: Only as far as it concerned their own safety. In exchange for the high price the US paid for NATO, the European countries could have supported the US by creating an absolute standardization from the beginning. They did not. The first armored vehicles The Netherlands and Belgium bought, were the lousy AMX from France. If we turned a bit too quick to the left, the vehicle did, but the right track continued its journey straight ahead. When The Netherlands needed a tank hunter, it turned out to be the AMX 75 with a 110 barrel. After five rounds the turrets were torn up. When we bought tanks, it was leopards from Germany. When Belgium bought F-16, the US had to buy in exchange the machine guns from FN. And when that F-16's needed an upgrade, it was done by Dassault in exchange for more than 100 Million BFr bribe for the different Socialist party leaders. When The Netherlands in the sixties needed new rifles as successor for the US M1 Garand, it were the FAL's from Belgium while with the tests the M-16 of Colt came better out of the tests. When in the nineties The Netherlands needed new rifles to replace the worn-out FAL's, they bought, indeed, M-16. But from Canada. When Belgium needed, after the 2nd world war, new jeeps to replace the US NEKAF's, it were Minerva's of Bombardier in Canada. Because Bombardier was French speaking. That the Minerva's, the kind of vehicle clowns use for their performance in a circus, did not meet the requirements of fighting units did not matter. The French bought nothing from the US and withdrew its military presence in NATO. The Norwegians had in the beginning launching vehicles and equipment for the Honest John, but did not allow nuclear weapons on their soil. Greece repeatedly threatened to quit NATO if it did not get what it wanted (against Turkey). It had the US to pay high prices for the use of their airfields. Spain joined NATO in the early eighties and wanted an Iberian command on its soil. Portugal decided that it would never allow one Portuguese under Spanish command. Spain did not get his Iberian Command and restricted his NATO membership immediately to the political part. This all might be called 'politics', it might be called 'commercial necessities', it might be called 'the independent European course within NATO', it was, in some cases proven, bribery. And in the proven cases French and Italian bribery. I don't even dare to think about the not-proven cases. As this letter is not a lesson in terrorism and history, it is not a lesson in bribery.

Of course the economical factor of the presence of the US forces in Europe may not be neglected. The US sold many weapon systems to Europe, beginning with the Super Sabre and the M-1 carbine and ending with the F-16 and the YPR 765. But it always had to accept compensation orders. And the Belgian politicians preferred to be corrupted by Dassault and Augusta, the French permanently tried to play a role in a 'European fighter' and we might say that the only standardization in NATO was, for a long time, the air in the tubes of the vehicles. When Plans and Policy Section of LandA at SHAPE in 1982 launched his SHAPE Guidance for Stockpile

Planning in ACE, it turned out that no country ever tried to meet the 30 day requirements. Closest to it were the US, UK, Germany and the Netherlands. And when SACEUR, Gen Rogers, mentioned that during a visit to the Dutch parliament, the general opinion in that parliament was:"Wie denkt die brutale Amerikaan wel dat hij is." Or, in good American:"Who the fuck thinks this Yankee that he is."

You don't believe that? Ask the intelligence file of that period. I know it. I typed and corrected the presentation for Col. Tudor CCF, Chief Logistic Readiness Center of Ops Div at SHAPE, and read the reactions at that time in the Dutch newspapers.

Looking into the present situation and asking: Should the US remain member of NATO? the answer in my opinion is NO. Let them try to find back those dentures and develop out of that WEU a European defense force. The US is far better situated without NATO.

4: Quit the UNO

The establishment of the UNO was meant to prevent war. Nice. Since that establishment after the 2nd world war we have seen continually and increasingly wars in this world. In fact the UNO was, and is, the most powerless bunch of good-for-nothing politicians the world has ever seen. Some remarkable observations:

■ The official languages of the UNO are English and French. The latter cost only a lot of money that could have been spent for better purposes than to satisfy the pretension of being important of a country that has kept, and keeps, corrupt dictators in his former colonies in Africa in power. France is far from the equal of the US.

- The UNO never refused a dictator to be present in the assembly.
- The Director-General never corrected a speaker after the man had almost openly offended the US for one reason or the other.
- The UNO never condemned the Islam for committing the gruel habitude to commit genital mutilation on young girls.
- The UNO never condemned Saudi Arabia, Morocco, Iran and Afghanistan for committing discrimination of Christians.
- The UNO never condemned massacres, committed by Muslims, with Christians as victims.
- The UNO, after recognizing Israel, never condemned the whole Arabian world in the Middle East for their permanent terrorism in Israel or for their hate campaigns against that country in the schools.
- The UNO allowed M'Bow of the UN in Geneva to commit favoritism for a long time (till the US acted and refused to pay his contributions as long as M'Bow was in function.
- The UNO never avoided a war.
- The UNO never enforced its resolutions
- The UNO pays much to high wages (See Pronk) to their servants, thus parasitizing on the people for who the money is really intended for
- The UNO was not capable of convincing the people in Africa that goats are the most destructive livestock for their dwelling-places and the environment.
- The UNO was not capable of avoiding an outburst of AIDS in the world and then especially Africa and Asia.

As with the other subjects, I could continue ten other pages of shortcomings, weaknesses and impotence of the organization. If they have done any good, it escaped my attention.

Fact is that the US, using its UNO-contribution in its own way, could do much more good and with better results and, what is more, on its own conditions.

The US do not need this money-absorbing organization and should quit the UNO and expel the organization from US territory. I am sure that the UNO will be reduced to a debating club as NATO would be after US withdraw and the main subject would be whether the new UNO headquarters would be located in Paris or in Moscow. Welfare of the poorest in the world would be item number 5 million on the agenda

5: Back to the roots

Back to the roots does not mean regression. The US is a country with a vivid imagination, an economical potency that challenges and influences the economies in the world and a military potency capable of defending its interests all over the world.

- Unfortunately the vivid imagination these days is restricted to well known females, movie stars and artists who became well known by spreading their legs, pushing all kinds of unspeakable things between them and then writing a book to explain how and why they did it and hoping that the book will be a bestseller. For what is called a fairly puritan country this is a shame. In fact it is a shame to every country. But it is much more a shame to the US because it provides the US with a soiled image. I once defended a USAF sergeant who was threatened to be dismissed from the USAF because, as a very young man, left alone without any guidance from a superior and unmarried, had a love affair with the spouse of another US NCO. I requested his commander not to have the young man fired because he did nothing wrong. This commander answered that adultery was unacceptable within the USAF. I told him that the forces of a country reflect the habitudes of its habitants and that the US is filled-up with movie stars that commit adultery, that divorce is the first cause of split-up marriages and not dead-by-old-age as it should be and that those days the most disgusting movies from the US were distributed around the world. In such a society adultery was not objectionable. The commander agreed with me that it happened but that is 'not done' in the USAF. Nevertheless, he was willing to accept my statement that the young man was left without guidance and the sergeant was not fired. But the affair shows exactly how the citizen of the US feel and what they do. Of course the main part of the Americans are normal people, with a normal lifestyle and loyal to their family. But what is seen in the world are the questionable movies, the glamour magazines with their pictures of rebuild bodies of the kind of movie stars who write books and their ridiculous marriages. The US government should realize that America's image in the rest of the world does not depend on what they do well to the world but on what the world see of the US. Every citizen in the US should be more aware of the impact of his behavior on the opinion of the world. Besides, that kind of behavior does not fit a country that requests God 'to bless America'. Also the image of a Coca-Cola drinking and fast-food eating bunch of computer freaks is something to think about. Americans **drink** Coke and **eat** fast-food. Microsoft **is** the leading software producer. But half the world does and relies on the results of the work of that computer freaks and imitate them. If I compare a T-bone steak with that terrible boiled frog legs I know what to choose. But the US has been marked as and has the image of an uncultivated country with overweight people, caused by the consumption of hormone stuffed meat, a bad social climate, permanently in a hurry, a high crime rate and every four years an election circus, while the European countries are displayed as countries who are known for their fine cookery, an ideal social climate, an excessive control on their food, a successful program to control the use of drugs, a reasonable and humane prison regime and very serious and worthy election system. The media forget to tell that our fine foodstuff has been and is almost permanently contaminated by the most deadly diseases and poisons, a social climate in which fraud is committed to such an extent that the whole system is endangered, drugs turned out to be an uncontrolled problem so the countries stopped the prosecution of violators, the prisons are that much overfilled that criminals are send home or are not anymore sentenced to prison penalty and the many elections are preceded by the most disgusting and a-social negotiations between the politicians to divide the available, well paid, jobs and create more posts to fulfill the demand for sources of income for their political allies. I am convinced that the anti-American publications are not a governmental issue (besides France) but it is benevolent allowed by the different governments. The US should do more about its image to the world. A program on the schools that makes the young females more aware of the word dignity, that encourages to develop more social control between the youngsters, that give them another view on what the commerce tries to do with them concerning their clothes (That marvelous angora sweater of the fifties covered more and had much more sex-appeal than the foolish, nothing-hiding clothes girls are forced to wear because there is nothing else.) and their behavior, that mutilation of the body by piercing is a disgusting way to express oneself, that tattoos are the proud of seamen and soldiers and that, from the moral point of view only they are entitled to wear them, that there are other windows on the future than movies full of violence and sex. That the choice of a husband supposed to be one for life so it has to be a careful choice, That a produced bastard is still a bastard after the mother marries someone, that excessive behavior with drugs and alcohol is to be loathed. The US should take more care of what is written in foreign newspapers and should, via advertisements, react on negative articles. The US newspapers should pay much more attention to the shortcomings of countries that allow, without any reason and much too strong colored comments, critics on the US and his organizations and citizen. On articles and comments in Newspapers in which people claim that, and this occurred really as a comment on the terrorist attacks (Het Laatste Nieuws), the bombings of Hiroshima and Nagasaki, The Vietnam War were also terrorist attacks, the US should by means of his local Ambassador immediately demand rectification and an historical oversight of the historical events of minimum one page. If the government of the country in which it happened does not obey, the Embassy of that country should be closed. I am convinced that it will not take long before the countries understand what the US is teaching them. I am also convinced that with a good combination of programs the image of the US outside the US will be much better within a few months. And, what is as important as well, people will better understand what the United States of America, as a country, as a habitat for its citizen, as a 'way of life', as that 'notion' I mentioned, really is.

■ The economical power of the US is, has been and will be in the future the worry of most of the governments in this world. The US has the most voluminous import of all countries, the dollar is still the international currency and the technological qualities are still unbeaten. On the Kyoto conference the US was, by the Dutch socialist politician Pronk, accused of being the biggest consumer in the world. Imagine, Mr. President, what would happen to Europe, Japan and China had you answered:"Yes, you are right. We are ashamed to spend so much money to buy French wine and delicacies, Dutch flower-bulbs and cheese and Heineken, German sausage and beer etc. and from now on, I promise you, we will import nothing from all that countries anymore to avoid the environment of Japan, China and Europe being spoiled." I can assure you, Mr. President, that Pronk would have been lynched by a committee of the ministers of economical affairs of the countries concerned. Of course the US is a consumer country. That is why so many emigrants went from the whole world to the US. To enjoy **that** part of the American way of life. And the countries exist, in the economical sense, of your import. If they accuse the US of causing world-wide environmental pollution, they have to blame themselves because they produce all that export goods. I always wondered if the US was really depending on the import. I don't believe that. The US is perfectly capable of maintaining its own economy. The US should, economically, rely more on itself and less on countries that are, when it comes to the points of loyalty, support when necessary and back-up in every sense of the word in times of peril, not very trustworthy. Up till now the European countries have always tried to find ways to diminish import from the US. They do it by taxes, by foodstuff laws, by making US products unknown, on cultural bases and by

143

making US products subject to suspicion. US meat may not be imported because of the use of hormones, but the hormones mafia in Europe is one of the most successful organizations existing and we had already contamination by PCB in cattle food, the Creutzfeld-Jacob disease and some other diseases that invariable always were to late reported to the European Commission. I buy my jeans and other clothes via a catalog warehouse in the US. I care that the material as well as the fabrics are 'made in the USA' to avoid inferior materials. By that means I have better fitting clothes (more sizes), a better quality and, even with the costs of transport and import taxes and TVA, I buy much cheaper. But I cannot buy a levis- jeans because, forced by the Europeans, catalog warehouses are not allowed to export from the US to Europe any Levis goods. The French are afraid for US influence in France. So they ban, as often as is possible and with the most illogical reasons, US films and books in the original language. (Ever heard a cowboy speaking French in a western movie? Really ridiculous). This kind of attitude towards US exports is general in Europe. China and Japan are producing mass goods for export and usually to the US. But they have their imports from the US always kept to a minimum. Was it not possible to produce those goods in the US? Is it not anymore possible to produce Studebakers instead of Toyota's? Does a factory employee really cares whether he produces a US car instead of Toyota or Nissan? I believe that a program that promotes US-styled and US-produced goods should cause a better balance between imports and local fabrication. Free world trade sounds good, but if the other countries hamper your export with the most ridiculous tricks like "Language", 'To expensive" etc. and children-labor is used, competition falsification is the word you are looking for and US economy will never reach an average level. The present economical level of the US is just good for every country except for the US. It is the interest for all that countries to keep it that way. And it keeps the US in a vulnerable position. Balancing on the needle of mercy of other countries. It's time to change the US attitude of the rich uncle to that of the old council of the Dutch United East-Indian Company.

- **Better to have an honest enemy than an unreliable friend.** That is one cliché. **Looking for your enemy? Kill your best friend.** That's another. **In a country where guns are outlawed, only outlaws will have guns.** That's American. And all the three fit the US.

- The US was the initiator and enthusiast supporter of the many treaties, regulations and resolutions of the UNO. Indeed, the world would be a better world if everybody obeyed those regulations. There would be no war, no starving, education for everybody, Christian churches next to the Muslim sanctuary in Mecca, a sovereign Tibet, Israel living within safe borders, equal races, and equal rights for women and no terrorism. Hey, what's that? Yes, no terrorism. But the US believed in a world that would live after the regulations of the UN. The rest of the world did not. So the US has itself positioned in the situation of an honest, martial-arts trained civilian who obeys the laws and has no arms. **And who was murdered by an armed criminal who did NOT obey the law.** The 20th century ethics which led to the UNO and its regulations is nothing more than the result of the thoughts of some philosophers and politicians, of that early fifties, of how the world should function as a combination of many countries with all their political, religious and cultural differences. That does not necessarily make those thoughts and its results the most logical or fitting the real character of all this nations, the tribes in that many nations and the visions on the future of many, not in the decision process involved revolutionaries. It even did not fit in the vision of the Soviet Union, France, the UK, and Belgium. Portugal or The Netherlands by that time. The first was an expanding imperial dictatorship based on extreme idealism. The latter were colony holders with no intention to give-up their profitable protectorates and thus sources of welfare in the homelands. So there may be some doubts about their intentions. If Sukarno was by that time for the Dutch a criminal, he is now remembered as the man who finally liberated Indonesia from the Dutch, thus being a hero. That counts for many other freedom fighters, all over the world, as well. Since the establishment of the UNO many wars for freedom and sovereignty occurred and men, who were by that time called revolutionaries and criminals are by now honest politicians. Many of them are proud on what they did and would not like to be remembered of the throats they cut, the women they raped and the children they murdered. If you think this is history, just remember the ten Muslim women who were found, swaying on meat-hooks, in the cold storage room of a hospital somewhere in Bosnia with their matrix cut open, the unborn babies taken out and cats sewn in. Maybe those kinds of happenings do not meet the ideals of the UN. But it is as the world itself. And in this world the US has, with other well-meaning nations, given his word that it will obey the regulations of the UN. The US has developed the best organized, most sophisticated and probably best trained forces in the world. And then decided to have the use of this forces, its safety and the future of the country depending on a bunch of former throat-cutters who became honest politicians and negotiations with heads of states who think first of their own welfare, than of their positions within their own countries and finally of their own people. And this all based on the thoughts of some philosophers and politicians who had a weak moment and considered wishful thinking to be the ultimate level of their extraordinary spiritual capability.

As with the economical regulations, the US obeys the UN regulations while others do not. It is for the US 1 minute to twelve. It is time that the policies of the US are adjusted to the real situation in this world and not to that as we hoped it would be.

By this time you might ask yourself what all of this has to do with you first problem, namely the war against terrorism and your primary goal, namely getting Bin Laden at his throat.

Let's consider it in that order.

FIGHTING TERRORISM

Terrorism is a wide spread phenomenon that stretches from a husband that forces his depending wife, by his physical power, to things she does not want and the strongest boy on a school yard who forces his classmates to do as he wants to official and by the UN recognized regimes who force the subjects of occupied countries to live according to the laws of that regimes. For India the Muslim freedom fighters in Cashmere are terrorists. For Pakistan it are indeed Freedom fighters. And this situations are found everywhere on the world. In general, the leaders of this kind of revolutionary groups are no more than ordinary gangsters looking for power and personal profit. But in many cases the UN recognizes them as having 'certain rights'. On the other hand, this people do not recognize the regulations of the UN. Did they, then is would be perfect possible that, during elections, they were not voted for. So it may be said that, if they do not get what they want, they terrorize the population in a certain territory to force them out of the area. This is not only taking place in Sri Lanka, Cashmere, Bask country in Spain, Ulster in the UK and Turkey with its Kurdistan. It also happens in many cities in Europe, where immigrants in the poorer quarters of the towns, once they are settled, terrorize the local population, by cutting their tires, throwing a stone through a window, putting household waste in front of their doors or, in groups simply staring at them when someone leaves his house. Invariably a local habitant tries to sell his house, which usually happens to a much to low price. The house is bought by, indeed, a member of the same ethnic group as has forced the family out. Also this is terrorism.

Complains usually turn out in accusations of racism, discrimination and offense and local politicians do not react. It is not strange that in many countries in Europe Neo-Nazi groups exist by which Hitler was a simple left-wing party leader.

Bin laden is in fact nothing more than a local habitant in a Muslim country who saw 'American' influence as being a threat to Muslim lifestyle. That his activities force his family to drop him is much more a matter of fear than condemnation.

And now you have to fight this kind of man.

If your special forces ever get him alive, you cannot do else than transport him to the US, and try him. The flow of events is easy to foreseen. A whole bunch of lawyers, even US lawyers, will take care of him, will claim that he is not out of free will in the US, is not according to the UN regulations delivered by the nation in which he was arrested and finally, when it comes to trial, the evidences might not be sufficient to condemn him according to your own laws. And then he walks out free. Afghanistan will demand the US to pay for all the damage in that country, caused by the bombings and the UN have to agree with them because he was found innocent during the trial **IN THE UNITED STATES.** Of course the entire Muslim world will be enjoyed and President Bush goes into history as the republican version of Carter.

As I mentioned before, the treaties with the UNO, NATO and your own laws will beat the US. The reason of existence of these organizations is old-fashioned. One good point is that many countries with mixed religions, especially when the important minority is Muslim, fear for religious fights. So you will have countries on your side. If not for friendship, than because of fear. There are also millions of foreigners (Non-US individuals) who consider themselves on moral grounds obligated to the US. I never gave myself the credit to be the only one. The US has many friends. The US will not be left alone when the following things would happen:

1: NATO
NATO is standing behind the US and article 5 applies. Let them prove their willingness.
A: Request **ALL** NATO partners a proportional contribution with a minimum of one Fighting Battalion to one Division **under command, not under operational command**, for a ground operation in Afghanistan.
Motivation is that you don't want civilian casualties.

B: If this request is refused (and it will be refused), withdraw without any comment all US forces from Europe, from NATO, from all headquarters and installations with all their equipment. (It will be clear that the means for transport have to be ready and prepared before the request is done) except from the countries that were willing to deliver the requested units and stop every financial contribution to NATO.

C: Denounce the NATO treaty.

D: Don't pay one dime anymore. Countries like Belgium with an important presence of US military men on their soil with all their rented housed and many local wage employees will appeal to their laws to make you pay for broken contracts etc. Don't react.

E: Declare all military representatives on the NATO-country Embassies in Washington Personae Non-Grata.

Consideration:

NATO is losing its value in a rather quick tempo. All countries that want to be members (former Warsaw-pact countries) do not want that for security reasons but for economical reasons because they know they will never meet the NATO requirements and want NATO to pay for it. The present members have made their contributions already a hollow trunk. Many countries can't get their armies filled-up and are not capable of recruiting enough solders for fighting units. See enclosure one and mark the date. Unfortunately this is Dutch, but I am sure that it can be translated.

After the denouncement of the treaty and the persistent silence from the US, you may expect a serious diplomatic offensive. That should be ignored totally. Also your ambassadors should not react. I don't believe that one country will dare to put any pressure on your ambassadors.

The rest of the world will be amazed, fidgety and speculating on what the US is up to.

In view of the new policy that the US will not allow any country to offend the US, his people or his President or allow any anti-US article in any newspaper, it is important that the staff of the US embassies collect all publications in the local newspapers. It will be a lot.

2: UNO

A: Call the Assembly of the UN together to address them.

B: Demand from the concerned countries that all terrorist who committed their crimes against the US and its subjects be delivered to the US within two weeks.

C: Demand that all countries obey completely and without hesitation the Human Rights Treaty.

D: Demand that the waste of funds, by using French as a second official language be stopped. Point out that there would be much more reasons to use Chinese, Russian, Spanish or German because of the amount of people who use those languages.

E: State that the Islam with its education system that cultivates a hate to every other religion and every other lifestyle caused the many terrorist attacks and is responsible for it. Demand that the total of the damage, the material damage as well as the economical damage afterwards be paid for within one month after this day.

By the time you have come that far, a storm of verbal indignation will fill the assembly. You will probably not be able to address them further. Have the demands of the US be visible on a screen by then and leave with your party (preferably Minister Powell, if he can be convinced, Mr. Al Gore to prove that it is the whole of the US who is standing behind you and one US marine of the lowest grade in service dress who will stand next to you without any movement) This fighter must be the last one to leave. He must be capable of putting an expression of absolute disdain on his face towards the yelling crowd of former throat cutters, dictators, cowards, hangers-on and former unreliable allies before he turns around and closes the door behind him.

I am convinced that you will get no positive answers on your demands. There is no doubt that the whole world expected something spectacular after quitting NATO. They will never have dreamed that you would dare to such an action. But the world will realize that your demands are serious and that you will quit the UNO when they do not comply with that demands.

Again, your embassies will have to make overtime to collect all nasty remarks concerning the USA and especially its President.

Again there will be a lot of diplomatic activity

Wait till the deadline of the ultimatum concerning the demands is passed.

Quit the UNO and have all that too well paid people removed from US territory.

Declare, according to the US laws, war against an unknown enemy.

By this time you know who your real friends are, have started negotiations on bilateral agreements with the countries that are at least not hostile in their attitude towards the US and his President or have the same interests and remove your Embassies from all hostile countries.

By this time the total world will be aware that you really want these terrorists, that the concerned countries have no choice, that the world is changed and, to quote a Japanese Admiral after the attack on Pearl Harbor, that they have woken-up a tiger.

The pressure on you to have Bin Laden arrested and stop terrorism will change to those who know where he is and how to get him. Fearing for the results of the US withdraw from all important organizations and possible US boycotts against their countries, the world will turn against the pro Bin Laden countries and force them to deliver him to you. You might very well get Bln Laden as a present with the holy Kaa ba from Mecca as an extra. Am I dreaming? Not at all. History has proven that Arabian honor is a whipped-up emotion that melts down immediately when their property is in danger. Honor means nothing to those who consider the contents of their wallet more important than anything.

THE UNITED STATES PROGRAM AFTER THE UNO
1: Self supporting
When the USA declared war to Japan and Germany, one of the first things that changed was the transfer from peace economy to war economy. But by then the US was quite self-supporting. By now the US depends on imported oil from countries that are hardly reliable and absolutely not loyal to the US without any restriction. Their loyalty depends on Dollars. And that counts for many countries with other

natural sources to be imported by the US. So if you declare war to an unknown enemy, a war economy is indispensable. In this case not because so many products, weapons etc. have to be produced, but to make the US absolutely independent of foreign suppliers. This should start with:

A: The acquirement and stockade of as many raw materials and half fabricates of any kind as is necessary to economically survive any boycott. In fact the US should have a strategic reserve for several years to cover the results of B.

B: A research program that searches for new sources of energy and the enlargement of the US capability to use alternative sources of energy and production of artificial substitutes for any of the kind of raw materials the US industry needs to import.

C: Reduce the import of foreign luxury goods to a minimum to make the country aware that the US can only rely on the US and to reduce the import debts.

D: Militarize the research for medication. The US may expect other diseases to be contaminated with by terrorists.

E: Isolate in camps, as has been done with the US citizen from Japanese origin after Pearl Harbor, all Muslims in the US. Have them **all** interrogated with use of the Truster Program or any other quick result giving means and pick out the rotten individuals, US citizen or not. The results of these interrogations might very well be surprising for your citizen.

I am convinced that many countries will choose the side of the US and will be very willing to continue the already existing cooperation. There is hardly any change that you will even find a country that objects the US. Not only because they fear for economical damage, but also because they fear for the alternative: a possible political take-over by fundamentalists of any kind of religion or political idea. Nevertheless, governing is looking forward and a good military habitude is that if you see any possibility for an enemy to act somehow, one has to take measures to hamper that.

2: Military

The present defense system of the US might be sufficient or not, but a reinforcement of the forces should be considered. Especially those who guard the frontiers. Besides that, the forces should be extended with sufficient units of sufficient specialist to be capable of executing the following tasks:

A: Intrude in hostile countries as well as friendly countries to find, arrest and transport to the US any terrorist, those who assist him, relatives and/or friends who are wanted by the US or can be used as hostage to get necessary information to find, arrest or destroy other terrorists and their installations. In this case an explanation and an example might be enlightening.

Terrorist of the non-suicide type are usually cowards. They fear most that what they do to others. That is how their fantasy works (Bullets and knives). If Arafat was arrested and told that he was getting the same treatment as that US Marine Colonel in Lebanon if he did not betrayed the killers of that Colonel, he would be reduced to a psychological wreck. Men with that kind of lips are not strong. I am convinced that you would not need to hang him.

In the Second World War, a small party of freedom fighter (terrorists from the point of view of the Germans) ambushed Lt.Col Rauter, Chief Security Forces of the SS in The

Netherlands. They hurt him and killed his driver, an SS-soldier. Rauter was angry, of course he was. But he had understanding for what they tried to do to him. And he was furious that they killed his driver. The man was simply a driver and had nothing to do with the work of Rauter. Rauter arrested all males, from the youngest baby to the oldest man to a total of 400 in the small village of Putten, where the ambush took place, and announced that no one would be harmed and should be free again, that he would not take any other action against anyone if only the terrorists who committed the ambush would surrender.

They never did and 400 babies, children, adolescents and men disappeared in concentration camps to be seen never more. Up till today there is reason to believe that the freedom fighters did not come from the village of Putten. In this 400 were no relatives of them involved. But what if one of the sons, brothers or fathers was between the arrested? I believe that the involved individual would have been killed by his companions to avoid being betrayed by him.

No one ever claimed that ambush.

This kind of actions, as of Rauter, by the US would, after a while, be known by the world and would cause much more hesitation to commit terrorist actions.

B: Reconnoiter and set-up remote-controlled devises that eventually destroy installations which are important in the economical, political and/or military sense for the concerned country. Explanation:

The oil winning installations of Aramco are important to the US, but also to Saudi Arabia who is at this moment a 'friendly' country. But what to do if the country becomes hostile? You might consider it necessary to stop Arabian oil production. Already by now it is difficult to deploy forces somewhere if countries do not want to cooperate and military action might cause unnecessary losses. Is it not easier to ask your military Aide de Camp:"My dear Bill, is number 20 ready?" Answer:"Positive, Mr. President." And then push the button.

In fact this kind of devises should be placed on thousands of possible targets like military installations (not the weapons and stocks, but the conference rooms and command centers), parliaments, hotels where VIP's usually are housed, military harbors to block them, important industrial facilities and all other places of which your advisors consider it to be important to control their existence.

Is this also terrorism? Of course not. It is precautionary measures. 6 million Jews would have praised the man who would have killed Hitler in 1931. Only God knows how many Indians would praise the man who would have strangled Columbus. The total of the Dutch population would adore the man who would have cut the throat of King Philip the 2nd in the 16th century. And maybe 950 million Christians would have prayed straight into Heaven the man who would have called Mohammed a fantast and a liar and then kill him when, 1400 years ago, he came out of his tent and claimed to have been instructed by Allah to establish the Islam.

The President of the United States of America has the right to take precautionary measures to protect his country, his population and the integrity of the US against hostile nations and those nations who may become hostile.

Mr. President, you might wonder why I, as a Dutchman and serving my country in all senses of patriotism for such a long time, recommend this. The explanation is simple and straight. Holland has been, and is, loyal to the US and the objectives of the free world. It is expected that within some years the influence of the Muslim community is that important that Holland will be only Holland in name. It will not be anymore the Holland I served, the Holland with the mentality, the objectives and the free and democratic attitude I served. It will be a foreign country to me. And that is maybe the moment you might consider Holland to be hostile. It would be hostile to me as well.

I don't idealize the US as a heaven on earth. I only believe that, without the US, its way of thinking, its objectives and its open culture, the world would be a bad place to be. Europe and the world owe the US at lot. For me and many other millions the US means the last barrier between us and a dark planet.

C: Act as reporters of Newspapers, as authors, as historians or whatever their motivation may be to interview politicians, leaders of so-called peace organizations, appropriate members of churches and non-Christian religions, leaders of extreme political parties and other organizations. The interviews should be recorded to test the sincerity of the man by the Truster Program. This serves two purposes.

a: Is the man a danger to the US.

b: Does he know more of certain activities directed against the US.

Explanation:

If I would pretend to be an author who wants to write a book about the history of the Islam in Holland and be allowed an interview with a Mullah, I would start with asking him his own past. For instance why he wanted to be a mullah, how he was educated, if his family is with him, how he likes Holland etc. The questions might then be more directed to his work in the Mosque and the religious education he provides for the children, if he discussed with them the events of the 11th of September etc.

Since I am not a specialist in interrogation I really cannot say what kind of questions should be used. But I am certain that the series of questions can be developed by specialist who also can analyze them. The Truster Program shows exactly when the man lies and out of that analyze the knowledge of the man can be discovered. If this is done with thousands of people, it might be very well that you decide to use the kind of unit as described in A.

In general, an organization as described above should, if it does not already exist, be established.

3: Economical
Quitting NATO and the UNO does not automatically means that from one moment on the other the US loses his real friends. Nor will it lose its economical contacts with these friends, neither with neutral countries. Even more or less hostile countries will be very careful with quitting any contact with the US. There is one good reason for that. Everybody has to eat and if the people do not get their usual 2400 Kcal. daily, they might get a bit fidgety. No government in this world can afford a troubled population just because that government feels a bit corrected by the government of the country that provide them with that daily 2400 Kcal. by means of their export.

So there is no immediate danger for a lack of the necessary imports from the rest of the world.

When the world calms down again, governments will start bilateral negotiations a.s.a.p. to assure a flow of export to the US and a flow of Dollars from the US. I did say that the US should adapt the attitude of the former United East Indian Company to arrange his affairs in the future.

The VOC as it is called, never really occupied a place, a country or some piece of territory that belonged to someone. Its main goal was merchandise and making profit. If it could make that profit by exchange of goods, they only did it on the best, for them, possible conditions. It was willing to defend its property, like ships, real estate in foreign countries, support factories like Cape Town in South Africa, provisioning enclaves all over the world, but they never really caused hostile activities. There was one simple reason for that. Making yourself disliked means that you have to be prepared for hostile activities. Of course the leaders of the VOC were no fools. When they expected problems, precautionary measures were taken like equipping the ships with cannons when pirate activities were expected. Paying for a Dutch Navy and the establishment of a Marine Corps, attracting the best seamen like De Ruyter, Tromp, Hein etc. Officially they were admirals of the Dutch Navy and their task was the protection of Holland against England, France and Spain. But in fact all their activities served the purpose of protecting the interests of Holland at sea. And that interest was the free trade and best possible protection for the Dutch merchant vessels. It functioned for more than 250 years. When England by the famous Cromwell launched their Act of Navigation, Holland shrugs its shoulders and obediently greeted the passing English vessels first. For the VOC it was easier (and cheaper) than building more war ships.

In fact the US should adapt the same attitude. And that attitude means: We are a free country, we don't mix up in your business and you do the same or we will beat the shit out of you. It is also the same attitude of those men who conquered the West in the US.

An attitude like that means also that the theft of US knowledge, imitation of US products without license, unauthorized copying of US software, music etc. should be punished severe. The country that does allow it or does not prosecute should pay itself for those illegal activities. That means for instance that if a survey gives an estimate of 500 million Dollars of US losses in France, the French government should pay that money. If they want to get it recuperated, they should tax their citizen. In fact, by now in almost all countries in the world illegal software is used. The US today would have a profit of several billions of Dollars had it the possibility to force the countries to pay for what they connive at. And in fact you have that possibility but you don't use it. Illegal copying of software, products protected by patent and products that only pretend to be imported from the US but that are produced in low wage countries are forbidden. But the concerned countries gain by their production and claim to be not capable of doing something against it to stop it. But if from such a country all export is denied access to the US and the citizen of that country are expelled immediately, it might be that that country is willing to pay the estimated loss of money to the US because the economical damage might be much higher for them. And when one sheep is through the gate, others follow rather quickly.

It would be reasonable to negotiate with all countries with the condition: One Dollar in, one Dollar out.

Since you have, in this scenario, terminated all treaties, nothing stops you.

4: Policy

There is nothing wrong with the policy of the US towards the rest of the world. It is based on sovereignty, friendship, the will to improve the world to a better place to live for all human beings. I know that the US has changed a lot during the last 40 years. When I was a young seaman and with my ship sailing the US east coast, I saw that the harbor workers were not mixed. One hatch for the blacks, one for the whites. The toilets on the shore were marked 'black' or 'white'. During my last tour of duty at SHAPE I saw nothing more of that kind of things and had some excellent black and white US NCO's under command without any friction between them. This does not necessarily mean that the whole of the US has changed, but it has got a remarkable change in a rather short time.

The policy of the US to equal all individuals extends to the will to change the world in the same way. The western world has followed these ideas during the last 30 years.

In the time I was Marechaussee (1967 - 1972, we had NO black people in the Corps. A Marechaussee was tall, clearly of the Caucasian race, Christian, well educated and capable of enduring a kind of training and education that would make any super soldier jealous. The Corps was a military jewel and absolutely reliable. By now the recruiters are laying on their knees at the gates of the barrack, begging every possible recruit to join the service. The result is the same as with programming a computer. Rubbish in, rubbish out. That does not necessarily mean that the Corps is spoiled by black people. It means that the Corps is spoiled by recruits from dubious origin. Turkish and Moroccan youth, not adapted to western world values and hardly willing to accept them join the Dutch military services. Also the Marechaussee Corps. It proofs that our western values are not automatically accepted by other cultures. And the quick change in the US and the democratic western countries are too quick for those countries that had already a well developed culture when the US did not exist and my predecessors were chipping pieces of stone to make an ax. When the US and European countries initiated the founding of the UNO after the war, that treaty fitted only them. All other countries had totally other ideas about the international relations in the world. For the US and Europe, the world should be a free globe to every human being. For the Soviet Union, the world was not yet ready and MIR, according to their rules, should be established. For every Muslim Islam should rule the world (typical that Mir and Islam mean the same: PEACE). But that peace was for communists restricted to party members and for Muslims to males.

Fact is that the UNO treaty, its agreements and rules are based on the democratic values of the western world in which church and government are divided. And that does not function for Muslim countries, Hindu countries and dictatorships. The US idealism is as good as the real communist idealism. It does not work.

The present coalition against terrorism will last as long as you pay, as long as only Afghanistan is involved as victim and as long as other countries fear for an extending influence of the Islam. I can predict easily that this coalition will fall to pieces with the first attack on the next Muslim country.

There is only one solution.

The US should declare itself free from all former obligations, treaties, agreements and a law should pass that the US forces will never be used otherwise than protecting the US, its population and its interests. Never more will one member of the US forces die for anything else.

The US will never agree with a bilateral treaty that forces it to protect any foreign piece of territory

The US will base its international relations on bilateral agreements.

The US forbids foreigners to posses real estate, enterprises and influence in any US business, be members of US political organizations or any organization that might have any influence on the political decision making process.

The US allows every religion on its soil but forbids the genital mutilation of children. The school medical system checks this and parents who trespass this regulation are automatically condemned to penal servitude to earn the money to pay for the medical restoration on their account. They will be denied the parenthood over that child.

Every child must attend the official public schools. Schools based on a religion are not allowed.

The US government will not allow any country that has US citizen on its soil to prosecute or condemn them. In case of a committed crime, the US citizen must be, together with all evidences concerned, transmitted to the US for prosecution.

The US reserves the right to arrest, prosecutes, and condemns any person, irrespective of its origin, in case of any crime directed to the US or its interests.

The US reserves the right to claim the losses of such crimes from the country of origin of the condemned (They have to take care that such things cannot happen. If they fail, they have to pay.) These countries cannot use as an excuse that they have taken the nationality of the concerned criminal. The reason to take that nationality is also reason to arrest and deliver the criminal to the US, together with all his funds and properties.

I could carry on with, in fact, 500 amendments to the US Constitution, but by now the meaning should be clear.

The US is an independent country, possesses the most powerful military in the world and is capable of defending its interests, territory and integrity as a political entity in every sense and, if necessary, against the whole world.

5: Development aid

From the point of view of humanity, it would be cruel to stop helping the poor, the suppressed, and the people who deserve the right, by their fruitless efforts, on a better life.

But 50 years of development aid were not good enough to realize that under control of the UNO. Too much money is used as working funds for the organization itself. To less for the objectives. To many incapable, too well paid personnel was used and too many people needed too expensive Toyota's and Mercedesses, too big offices, too many personal assistants, too many experts who opposed each other. And the worst obstruction is maybe the rule that countries may not interfere in the internal affairs of other countries. That means that, how objectionable a regime may be, even with the best intentions another country may not interfere or, if necessary, finish the concerned regime. It means that development aid in many cases directly is transferred to the bank account of the involved president, dictator or whatever he calls himself.

If the US starts with the kind of schools as I propose (Enclosure 2) in a few selected countries and the US uses the money, that is wasted now for the UNO, for a development program for that few countries, using normal paid servants, such countries would adapt indeed a democracy and a lifestyle that enables them within a few years to join the western world on equal basis.

Many third world countries do not even posses such a thing as a government as the US thinks it should be. Many of those governments consist of not much more than gangsters with the attitude of chieftains of tribes.

Examples:

- The Belgian government calculated that Mobutu of Zaire possessed a personal fortune of 12 billion Dollars, sufficient to pay the national debt of the country. But where is the money now? The new ruler, Kabila, still asks for remittance of the debts and development aid. So that money must still be on those Swiss bank accounts.
- The different rulers with their civil war in Sierra Leone only fight for the possession of the diamond mines. They don't care about the population.

In both cases, personal gain is the motivation.

When the US takes a few countries under their wings, a program as follows might have success within four years.

Of course other countries will accuse the US to make clones of the US. You will remember what I advised to do with countries that make nasty remarks about the US.

The Program:

1- Select some appropriate countries, preferable with interesting natural sources for the US, and offer them your development solution **on your conditions.** Negotiations are not possible. It is a matter of: Take it or leave it.

2- Assign the best US-politicians from both the Republican Party and the Democrat party and persons who have a degree in political science to form a 'shadow' government and a 'shadow' parliament in the concerned country. These specialists should be mentors of the real government and parliamentarians.

3- Establish the schools as mentioned as well in the country of origin as in the US. The pupils who will attend the schools in the US should be the most promising. The working language should be English.

4- Develop a program of enlightenment for the population of the country that fits also illiterates.

5- Assign an average of all kind of professions, of course skilled men or women, appropriate for the expected economy of that country to assist in all kinds of enterprises to guide the personnel to a better and more economical way of working.

6- Develop and implement a medical service system that discourages abuse of the system, (as, for instance, in Europe where the system in many countries is abused to such an extent that the promotion of euthanasia became a must [Hitler would have adored it]) but is that good that people really have access to it to the reasonable price they can afford to pay.

7- Develop an education system that reaches **every** child and ranges from 6 year up to the 16th of the children.

8- Allow the appropriate youth to join the US forces with the purpose to promote the system as a basis for forces in the concerned country.

9- Encourage newspapers to appear and assure US newspapers available to those who read English. If necessary or desired establish a local newspaper in English. In schools, children should be forced to read newspapers by let them make abstracts of articles with their own comments on it. This totally separate from the schools I recommended.

10-   When the population has reached the level to make sound decisions on their own future, let the local and all that time monitored politicians draft a constitution that is:

- ■ Democratic
- ■ Fits the country
- ■ Displays the right of the individual
- ■ Describes exactly the moral standards the head of state should posses. (Nobody wants the disgusting trials as President Clinton had to endure thanks to his own behavior.)
- ■ Describes that the Head of state may have a salary up to 150% of the salary of the highest ranking commander of the forces.
- ■ Al the usual stuff that is in a constitution.

11-Announce elections for a new Head of state (preferable as is done in the US.)

12-Declare that the development work is done and withdraw all US personnel from the country.

The whole process is an intensive and much demanding affair, but after that 4 or 5 years, the US will have, depending on with how many countries it is capable of starting, a certain amount of reliable states that live with the same ideas.

Saying that this kind of states will be clones of the US is nonsense. The process will change, no doubt about that, the way of life and attitudes of the population. It will also relativize the importance of tribes and religions. But it never changes the typical behavior of someone who lives in a tropical country or contrary to that.

Such a program can only be successful if the US sees afterward to it that foreign multinationals don't take over the local economy. A more or less covered program via the still present local English newspapers can guide that.

Mr. President, I have not the arrogance of thinking that I can do what the whole Staff of the President of the United Stated cannot. Neither do I have the pretension to make you believe that I know everything. Contrary to that. But 33 years of service and a remarkable professional past taught me a lot about human behavior. I hope that many Americans will do the same as I did, namely writing their opinions and ideas down and send them to you. And I hope that you have a good computer program to sort this letters out and pick-up the ideas that might fit your policies and proposed actions.

I do not know whether God exists or not. I am raised in the typical Dutch way of Calvinism and, after intensive study, lost my faith. But if God exists, may He bless America.

Yours Truly,
C. Brouwer

EPILOGUE

Is there any arrogance in writing one´s thoughts and opinions in a book? If so, millions of people filling the social media like Facebook with their thoughts and opinions are. And very often their posts are not based on knowledge or experience but on feelings.

Donald Trump has won the elections and with that, offers the people of the United States new opportunities. And the most important one is to make "America great again". But making it great again is not a feasible task for one man. It is a task for the whole of the population. The difference in views on how the US should function in a world marked by religious violence and protect them is a task for specialists. The difference in views on how the people of America finds itself back as a nation in all its diversity of races, creeds, social feelings for each other and willingness to accept those values and defend them is a matter every American should answer for himself. To give content to it and willingness to accept compromises is a matter for all Americans. Donald Trump can only create the conditions for this. And he can only create those conditions if he is willing to listen to the people. That is not reading newspapers or following the social media by one of his Staff members, but inviting regularly ordinary people to The White House and go into discussions on issues that concern the whole community. And he'll have to do it personally. One afternoon of direct contact with people who are wherever and invited to follow a staff assistant immediately to such an event will teach Donald Trump more than a month of investigation by some specialist who then reports his results. That will always be average second-hand thoughts.

We must hope that Donald Trump is willing to accept advice and vision from his own ordinary countrymen and women. Can he? If so, then America will be ´great´ again after eight years.